Auguste Rodin

Cathedrals of France

Auguste Rodin

Cathedrals of France

Translated by Elisabeth Chase Geissbuhler

BLACK SWAN BOOKS

Originally published in 1914 as *Les Cathédrales de France* (Librairie Armand Colin)
Copyright © 1965, 1981 by Elisabeth Chase Geissbuhler.

*Published in co-operation with the Medieval Studies Program
at the University of Connecticut, and the Cultural Services
of the French Embassy in the United States.*

Revised edition
Published by
BLACK SWAN BOOKS Ltd.
P.O. Box 327
Redding Ridge, CT 06876
ISBN 0–933806–07–8

Contents

Preface

PARADOXICALLY, this is a book about sculpture. It is also a book about the great sculptor who wrote it, Rodin. He realized, as no sculptor since the Middle Ages had done, that the formal characteristics of sculpture and architecture are identical. Sculpture had no separate origin; architecture had no separate origin. From prehistoric times the two arts were as integral as the womb and the fetus. The life within and the shell without were molded by the same destiny, the same desire. Rodin was the first modern sculptor to understand this vital connection between the two arts and the greatness of his own work is a direct consequence of this understanding.

Rodin might have gone to Greece or Egypt for a confirmation of an intuition that had come to him in the course of his own development as a sculptor, but that was not necessary because there was ample proof in the churches and cathedrals of his own country, France. He loved her cathedrals and often stayed in their precincts, taking for preference a room that looked out upon the cloisters or the towers. In such circumstances he slowly composed this work, which is not a systematic account of these monuments—it is neither complete as a survey of all the Gothic cathedrals in France, nor an intensive study of a few representative cathedrals. Rather, it is a series of meditations on a profound experience, like Renan's famous prayer on the Acropolis, but more extensive, repeated for each cathedral and delicately differentiating between the separate impressions conveyed by each. Two preliminary chapters reveal the principles that are common to the construction of all these cathedrals, placing them in the setting of the French countryside and within the tradition of French art as a whole. The writing again and again rises to heights of eloquence that are essentially poetic, but it is always a poetry inspired by a sensuous contact with the living stones.

In using the word "impressions" I must not imply that there was anything vague or unrealistic in Rodin's approach to his subject. From the first page he begins to reveal his understanding of the technical problems that faced the master builders of the cathedrals, and beautiful is the way in which he immediately compares the movements implied by the structure of the cathedral to the compensations that establish equilibrium in the stance of the human body. This is but the first example of his realization of an organic principle that is implicit in all the arts and the secret of their enduring vitality.

Further, this same principle of organic unity (and always Rodin insists that unity is simplicity) gives to the arts their human and indeed their spiritual significance. Still within these preliminary pages Rodin tells us that in order to achieve an essential simplicity the artist must identify himself with the people, with the crowd, if he would produce a significant masterpiece: such masters must reclaim by the heart what they discover by the intellect.

Writing before the First World War, Rodin could even then complain of the indifference of the modern crowd to these great monuments of the past. "No one defends our Cathedrals." What would he have said if he had known that within the next thirty years some of his most beloved edifices would twice fall within the range of a devastating war? In a few hours the guns and bombs of the opposed armies had done more damage to Amiens, Soissons, and Reims than five centuries of neglect. Restoration and "redevelopment" have now done their equally deadly work, so that more than ever we are dependent on the sensibility of great artists such as Rodin to reconstitute the science and significance of our great heritage. Read how piercingly, how delicately this is done in the great essay on "Ornaments" (Chapter 13). Not even John Ruskin so faithfully, so lovingly, and so scientifically revealed the debt of the Gothic carvers to the flowering fields. From the same source, the master builder derived his sense of organic energy, expressed in that uniquely Gothic feature, the moldings of his stone vaults and piers. In this detail we see the power of the constructive intellect, and yet at the same time it is the tenderness of nature herself.

Finally there is that "Last Testament," which is one of the greatest affirmations that ever came from the pen of an artist: a hymn not so much to art as to life itself. I do not know what to compare it with, unless it be "The Song of Songs," for it too is based on love, the love of life, the love of God, and the love of the human form in which the artist finds this greater love embodied—"always the same splendor: always life recommencing and renewing itself with each pulsation." The cathedral conveys the same impression of "total astonishment," uniting body and soul, the finite and the infinite, in one precise intersection of forces. "A cathedral is a bond that unites us all, the pact of civilization"; and finally, listening to the Mass in Limoges cathedral, Rodin sums up all his theme in the one simple sentence: *Here all is love.*

Herbert Read

May, 1965

Translator's Note

IN THIS TRANSLATION, whose purpose is faithfulness to Rodin, only typographical ambiguities have been considered for possible change. One, but not the only one, concerns Rodin's personal capitalization.

As others underline words that reveal their passions, Rodin capitalized, but not invariably, those that stood for what he loved and, to a lesser extent, for what he abhorred. Of themselves these words indicate, as all Rodin's notes affirm, that he deplored the vices of the dawning industrial age: the denatured, mechanical, and systematic; while he adored all things of Nature and all that men make in loving obedience to her laws. Words also capitalized by religious writers, such as "Spirit" and "Grace," "Virgin" and "Mother," Rodin capitalized in reference to art and to Nature, while never precluding their religious significance. This was inevitable, since for him all art was sacred because its source, Nature, was sacred. Yet the word "art" is never capitalized in Rodin's writing.

The constancy with which that vital word is kept in lower case, contrasting with the inconstancy of his capitalization of all other words, may be understood as Rodin's refusal to elevate art separately from the transcendent Nature he venerated. Concerning the Romanesque he wrote: ". . . nothing is invented or willed by men who could have willed differently. All is interrelated. Creators are beings more obedient than others." Obedient, that is, to "Nature and her laws." Thus it is clear that obedient "art" should never be capitalized. But does it not follow that "Nature" always should be?

Unlike "Spirit" and "Grace"—capitalized alike when Rodin means gracefulness and one spirit continuing through the various art styles, as well as the Holy Spirit—the noun "Nature" in his writing always means the source of all art able to endure, thus always meriting his emphasis through capitalization.

In three articles he wrote for *Le Musée*, "Nature" is capitalized without exception, and in one four-page article, it occurs fifteen times. In this book, by contrast, "Nature" is capitalized only twelve times, and once is both capitalized and uncapitalized in the same sentence. In French, where there is normally less capitalization than in English, surely such inconsistency would have been corrected along with Rodin's spelling mistakes, had not editor, copy editor, and printer, warned of the great man's personal usage, been intimidated; they were not alone in this.

Both before and after 1910, when Charles Morice began assembling this book, Rodin's notes were passed among his admirers, many of whom were writers, and who might have made corrections. But comparison shows that however much he asked for help, Rodin firmly resisted change. We believe in the effectiveness of that resistance, we who are warned: "The laws that I express are those of instinct; they have no need of grammar, that children's nurse." With such warning who would reason with enigmas and risk falling into error far worse in Rodin's sight than inconsistency, the error of systematic capitalization, comparable to the sort of restoration by receipt that Rodin abhorred? Instead, everyone seems simply to have copied, as much for the original 1914 edition as for each one of the reprintings.

And after all, in this book made primarily of Rodin's private notes, it seems not unnatural to find words variably capitalized whose meaning and importance for himself Rodin's capitalization had established. So, however reluctantly for the word "Nature," Rodin's capitalization is followed here even to the omission of capitals for words he had previously capitalized, leaving the alerted reader free to make his own consistency.

E.C.G.

For their encouragement and advice,
the translator wishes to thank
Margaret MacKay, Alice Lewitin,
and especially Arnold Geissbuhler.

Auguste Rodin

Cathedrals of France

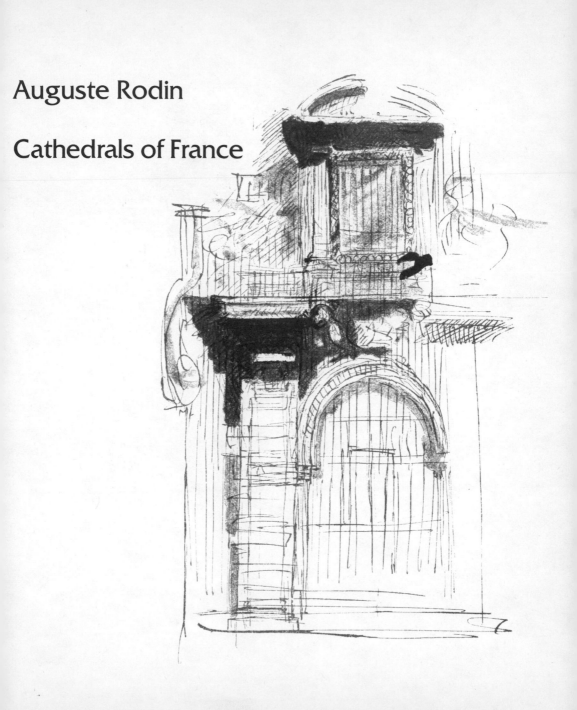

CHAPTER ONE

Initiation into the Art of the Middle Ages

I · PRINCIPLES · CATHEDRALS IMPOSE a sense of confidence, of assurance, of peace. How? By their harmony.

Here a few technical considerations are needed.

Harmony in living bodies results from the counterbalancing of masses that move. A Cathedral is built on the principle of living bodies. Its concordances, its equilibriums, exactly follow general laws according to nature's order. The great masters who erected these monumental wonders had complete knowledge of the science of their art and were able to apply it, having drawn it from its natural, original sources, because that science had remained alive in them.

Everyone knows that the human body, as it moves, changes its bearing and that equilibrium is reestablished through compensations. The leg that carries the weight when it comes directly beneath the body is the body's only pivot and makes, during that instant, the whole and unique effort. The leg that does not carry serves only to modulate the degrees of the stance, modifying the shift slowly, or rapidly if need be, until a new equilibrium is substituted, liberating the leg which bore the weight. In popular workingman's language this is called "untiring oneself," by shifting the body's weight from one leg to the other, just as a bearer might change his burden from shoulder to shoulder.

These indications are not without importance in relation to Cathedrals. The compensating movements, those perpetual and unconscious gestures of life, explain the principle that architects have applied in their flying buttresses which they needed to hold up solidly the enormous weight of their roofs.

And, as every rational application of a true principle has fortunate consequences in all domains beyond the immediate expectations of scholars and craftsmen, the Gothics were great painters because they were great architects. (It goes without saying that we use the word painter here in a large and general sense.) The colors in which these painters dipped their brushes are the light and shadow of day, and of the two twilights. The planes obtained by the great contrasts that the Cathedral builders had to find are of interest not only as equilibrium and solidity; they determine, besides, those deep shadows and beautiful blond areas that give the building so magnificent a vesture. For all holds together, the least element of truth evokes the truth as a whole, and the beautiful is not distinct from the useful, no matter what the ignorant may believe.

Those great shadows and great lights are carried solely by essential planes, the only ones that count from afar, the only ones that are not thin and weak because in them the half-tone dominates. And despite their power, or rather because of that power, those lines, those planes, are simple and without ponderance. Let us not forget that power brings forth grace; there is perversion of taste or perversity of mind in looking for grace in weakness. The details are designed to charm from nearby and to swell the contours from a distance.

Only effects of such intensity as this could carry to great distances. Thus the Cathedral arose to dominate the city assembled about her, as though under her wings, to serve as a rallying point, as a refuge to pilgrims lost along distant ways, to be their lighthouse, to reach living eyes during the day as far as the Angelus and Tocsin could reach living ears during the night. Nature also knows that perfect equilibrium of volumes is sufficient for the beauty and even for the grace of superior beings; she grants them only the essential. But the essential is all!

Thus the vast planes of Gothic monuments are engendered by the meeting of diagonal ribs which constitute what are called ogival arches. What elegance is in these simple and so powerful planes! Thanks to them, light and shadow react upon one another to produce half-tones, the principle of the opulent effect we admire in these mighty structures. This effect is entirely pictorial.

Here we have been led to speak first of painting in treating of architecture. Indeed this play, this harmonious use of night and day, is the end and the means, the very object and justification of all the arts. Is it not the whole task of architecture, that most intellectual and most sentient of the arts, the one which most completely requires all human faculties? Not in any other art do invention and reason take so active a part, but architecture is also the most narrowly ruled by the laws of atmosphere in which monuments are ceaselessly bathed.

The architect, as he works according to the laws that govern light and shade and according to his own intentions, has at his disposal only certain combinations of geometrical planes. But what immense effects he obtains by means so slight! May it be that in art effects are proportionately greater as means are more simple? Yes, since the supreme aim of art is to express the essential. All that is inessential is foreign to art. The difficulty is to untangle the essential from the nonessential. The more abundant the means, the more complex the difficulty, the more it becomes a delicate matter to do justice to the shades, the degrees of light that change hour by hour, without violating their natural liberty or betraying the thought one proposes to express.

Are not these supreme aims of architecture also those of sculpture? The sculptor who chooses his models from among living forms, from vegetables or animals, men or women, is indeed admirably served by the infinite variety of all that beauty; but this variety may also become a danger to him. He attains full expression only by devoting his whole study to the harmonious play of light and shade, exactly as does the architect. In the final analysis then, it is always by light and shade that a sculptor as well as an architect shapes and models. Sculpture is but one species in the immense genus of architecture, and we should never speak of sculpture without subordinating it to architecture.

How "masterpieces" are "masterpieces" I know, and what joy I have in knowing! In exactly the same way great souls are great souls. It is by rising to what is indispensable in the expression of their thoughts and feelings that both man and artist worthily fulfill themselves. A masterpiece is of necessity a very simple thing which comprises, I repeat, only the essential. All masterpieces would be quite naturally accessible to all men if they had not lost the spirit of simplicity. And even today, when people have become incapable of understanding, it is still with popular feeling, with a "soul of the crowd," that an artist must live to be able to produce a masterpiece.

He must feel with the crowd, be it but ideally present. He must understand this as the masters did. For the masters themselves became "crowd" in order to reclaim by the heart, by love, what they had discovered by intellect.

Gothic architecture, built in anticipation of the multitude and destined for the multitude, speaks the grand and simple language of masterpieces. The Cathedral guides light and shadow and governs them by means of the planes that receive those values. When one of two opposing planes is in light, the other is in shadow. Two such planes, already vast in themselves, grow greater still through opposition. The Antique is expressed by more shallow planes than the Gothic. Gothic planes are equal in value to the thickness and depth of their construction. But deep Gothic shadows are always mellow because they are maintained in the overall half-tone, that glancing luminosity which is the sun's loving caress.

There is little black in the Cathedrals. Black is used as a bold stroke which works destined to be seen in the open air do not seem to need. Our modern architects abuse the use of black; this is why all they make is so hard, so thin, so weak. The Renaissance style, which derives from the Gothic, uses black only as a mark of emphasis, while the half-tone dominates everywhere. Further, the bias plane of the arches, the flaring bell shape of the porches, the protruding frontal abutments, and in general all those planes that are in oblique relationship to the axis of the Cathedral, serve at once to enrich, to emphasize the unity of its grandeur and to produce the half-tone. One finds these oblique planes in the bas-reliefs, and even in the sculptured figures of arched doorways; this procedure is universal in the Gothic way of working, which accounts for the fact that the same sensitive and intelligent softness, accompanied by the same energy, prevails throughout.

I should like to inspire a love for this great art, to come to the rescue of as much of it as still remains intact; to save for our children the great lesson of this past which the present misunderstands.

In this desire I strive to awaken intellects and hearts to understanding and to love.

But I cannot tell all. Go and see. And above all, observe with a docile simplicity, consenting to work and to respect.

Let us study together.

II · WHERE shall we begin?

There is no beginning. Start where you arrive. Stop before what first entices you. And work! You will enter little by little into the entirety. Method will be born in proportion to your interest; elements which your attention at first separates in order to analyze them, will unite to compose the whole.

In the calm exile of work, we first learn patience, which in turn teaches energy, and energy gives us eternal youth made of self-collectedness and enthusiasm. From such vantage we can see and understand life, this delicious life that we denature by the artifices of our enclosed, unaired spirit, surrounded though we are by master-pieces of nature and of art. For we no longer understand them, idle despite our agitation, blind in the midst of splendors.

If we could but understand Gothic art, we should be irresistibly led back to truth.

How true, just and fertile was the method of our old masters of the 11th to the 18th centuries, a method which, in general and in union with all human forces of an epoch, is that of our own individual activities when they are well directed: the perpetual collaboration between man and nature.

Where indeed must this knowledge be sought? Everywhere. Look for it in the least, as in the greatest, of life's events, in our instinct as well as in our thinking.

Often one learns the most from things of modest appearance. Work is mysterious. It grants much to those who are patient and simple; it refuses those who are hurried and vain. It accords to an *apprentice* what it denies to the *pupil* of a school; and on a certain day the marvel is born out of the hands of a humble workman.

Where did I learn to understand sculpture? In the woods by looking at the trees, along roads by observing the formation of clouds, in the studio by studying the model, everywhere except in schools. And what I learned from nature, I have tried to put into my works.

By this means Gothic genius, after using the forests and the rocks, introduced into its masterworks the gardens, orchards, espaliers, and all the friendly farm vegetables, as well as all legends loved by the poor, together with all the most delicate details and most sublime episodes of life. And not content with borrowing from nature's beauties through constant, humble, and passionate toil in order to compose a festival of days, Gothic genius also assimilated the laws of natural creation to renew and perpetuate that festival by giving it variety. This is the sound method which enabled Gothic genius to express faint differences without contradicting itself and to continue to charm new generations.

Such variations are the transitions from one style to another.

With what supple grace, what wealth of invention, French genius moves from epoch to epoch to introduce a new phase in its architectural style! It disturbs nothing that already exists; it in no way contradicts the principles of the accomplished phase. *Order is followed* just as nature herself draws fruit from a flower. This is a transmission of life.

Both flower and fruit were models for the Gothics. One learns much by studying sequences, correspondences, and analogies—for the same law governs moral and emotional life—provided one already has an understanding of this general law. The Gothics had that understanding. But such discoveries are rewards. One obtains them only after many struggles, many steps over a long road, not counting detours made along side paths or meditative halts at crossroads.

Gothic art produced the French Renaissance by deducing from clear Gothic principles their consequences. Or to say that more accurately, the Renaissance is a Declension of the Gothic. It is, just as truly, the same Force which begets Grace and Spirit; it is a dream in several joyous tenses. The jubilant spirit uncoils into ornaments like a snake in the sun.

What a country this is to have possessed such vitality!

And to have conserved that vitality until our day of lassitude and lies when people consider adulterating old stones as well as old wines.

III · I KNOW that at the present time man is suffering; he invokes a change. A whole new world is stirring of which we know nothing, perceiving neither its proportions, its bounds, nor its harmony. Does Orpheus preside over the birth of this new world, or only that ancient Python who always expects to triumph over the eternally youthful Apollo?

However it may be, man has already known many changes before our time, and he has always known how to pass through them without sacrificing the past to the future. For all the weight of centuries, the Sphinx and the temples still raise their profiles of august serenity against the horizon. After Egypt and Greece, Rome has left everywhere the indelible imprint of its enduring and proud character.

Why has French architecture been tampered with?

Even today I can still see the Arena at Nîmes, but our Cathedrals are already more than half obliterated! Greece has indeed been mutilated but its sorrows and its wounds do not dishonor it. France has been slandered and reviled. That magnificent stone vesture, which might have been able to defend it against the future, has fallen into tatters at the merchants', and the odious fact neither irritates nor surprises anyone.

Will the genius of our race end by passing away like those pale ghosts and vanished forms that no one seeks any more? Was it in historical or mythical time that the Cathedral, rowing through space by its buttresses, all sails unfurled, the French ship, the French victory, beautiful as for Eternity, spread open at its apse the wings of a group of kneeling angels?

No one defends our Cathedrals.

The burden of old age crushes them, and under the pretext of curing them, of "restoring" what he should only uphold, the architect changes their features.

Crowds stop in silence before the Cathedrals, incapable of understanding the splendor of these architectural immensities, yet instinctively admiring them. Oh, the mute admiration of these crowds! I want to cry out to them that they are not mistaken; yes, our French Cathedrals are very beautiful! But their beauty is not easy to understand. Let us study them together; understanding will come to you as it has come to me.

And the means of understanding are all about you. The Cathedral is a synthesis of our country. I repeat: the rocks, forests, gardens, Northern sun, all these are condensed in this gigantic body. All of our France is in our Cathedrals, just as all of Greece is summarized in the Parthenon.*

Alas, we are at the evening of their great day. These forebears are dying, martyred.

Renan prayed on the Acropolis. Is no one tempted to praise you also, to protect you, French marvels, Chartres, Amiens, le Mans, Reims? Have we then no new poet to pray over our Cathedrals, those dolorous virgins, all stricken, yet all still sublime?

But architecture no longer touches us. The rooms in which we consent to live are without character. They are boxes crammed helter-skelter with furniture. Everywhere the "Conglomeration" style

* *Translator's note:* An extended version of this and the next two paragraphs appeared in Rodin's article for *Le Musée*, Revue d'Art Antique, Vol. II, 1905.

reigns. How can we understand the profound unity of the great Gothic symphony?

Those admirable workmen who, for having directed their thought to heaven, were able to fix its image upon earth, are no longer here to preserve their work. Day by day time steals a bit of its life, and restorers, by making a mockery of it, plunder its immortality. Evil days have come. Even such minds as a pure instinct inclines toward admiration, are not sure of understanding. Let us not blush for our lack of understanding! May our glory be in striving to understand. I declare to you that our architecture was the marvel of our marvels, the one among all which would have been worthy of universal admiration and gratitude, had we not dishonored it. Why indeed, when France will have gone into eclipse, her reign ended, may she not look forward to being judged by future generations according to her works and her merits? It would have been so fine to die as Greece died, to set like the sun inundating the world with light!

We shall have had neither the happiness of Athens, dying in its glory, nor that of Rome, leaving everywhere the ineradicable trace of its power.

The Gothics set stone upon stone, ever higher, not, as the giants did, to attack God, but to reach up to Him. And God, as in the German legend, rewarded the merchants and the warriors, but to the poet, what was granted?

"Where were you at the time of the distribution? I did not see you, poet."

"Lord, I was at your feet."

"Then sometime you shall come up beside me."

Thus it was the poet who guided the masterbuilder, and in reality the poet built the Cathedral.

The Cathedral is dying and with it the country, stricken and outraged by her own children. We can no longer pray before the humiliation of our supplanted stones. For living stones, scattered among bric-a-brac, dead things are substituted.

And yet, I cannot despair.

They still possess, despite all things and all persons, so much beauty, our old living stones! None has succeeded in killing them, and it is our duty to gather together and defend these relics.

Before I myself disappear, I wish at least to have told my admiration for them. I wish to pay them my debt of gratitude, I, who owe them so much happiness! I wish to honor these stones, so lovingly transformed into masterpieces by humble and wise artisans; these moldings admirably modeled like the lips of a young woman; these beautiful lingering shadows where softness sleeps at the heart of power; these delicate and vigorous ribs springing up toward the vault and bending down upon the intersection of a flower; these rose windows whose magnificence was inspired by the setting sun or by the dawn.

To understand Cathedrals one must be sensitive to the moving language of their lines, amplified by shadows and reinforced by the graduated form of their adorned or unadorned buttresses. To understand these lines, tenderly modeled and caressed, one should have the good luck of being in love.

It is impossible to be insensitive to the magic and virtue of all this splendor. What reserve of power and of glory might the new world find here? Though you transform the world according to your taste, there is at least one thing that will not change: that is the law which governs the relationship between light and shade and which, in their oppositions, creates harmony. The Gothics, following the Romans, understood that law.

When their masterpieces are no longer before our eyes, there will be nothing to remind us of that law.

When the death agony of our Cathedrals has been accomplished, our country will be transformed, dishonored—at least until that far-off time when human intelligence reascends to the eternal Beatrice.

IV · Who will come with me?

I am not traveling to Italy or elsewhere. For me, from my present point of view, the sky is the most important landscape. The sky reigns over all things, forever changing their aspect and making new spectacles of the most familiar sights.

And in fact, because I myself have changed, I find novelty in sights that are familiar, and beauty in forms that I did not understand before. My transformations come above all from my work: having studied ever more assiduously, I may say that I have ever more ardently and more lucidly loved.

As a young man, of course, I loved the Gothic lacework, but now I understand the part it plays, and I admire the power of that lace. It rounds out the profiles and fills them with sap. Seen from a distance, those profiles appear as delightful caryatids that cling to the framings like the vegetation that molds the severe line of a wall or console brackets that lighten the heaviness.

Little by little I have come to our old Cathedrals and have been able to penetrate the secret of their life as it is constantly renewed beneath the changing sky. Now I can say that I owe them my greatest joys.

Romanesque, Gothic, Renaissance! I know now that several long lives would not suffice to exhaust the treasures of happiness that our monuments of the past reserve for the sincere lover of beauty. And I am faithful to them. How often the snow, the rain, and the sun find me standing before the Cathedrals, like a French migrant worker.

In my pilgrimages I have had but few companions. Those I had were neither architects, sculptors, poets, priests, nor men of State, but foreigners who were verifying the statements of Baedecker.

Oh, why do you not recognize your true advantages? Why do you despise your good fortune?

Come let us study! Come and receive true life from those who are no more, but who have left us such magnificent testimony of their souls!

At each visit they tell me new secrets. They have taught me the art of using shadows as they should be used to envelop a work, and I have understood the lesson they give us in those full outlines which they always use. *The Cathedrals of France are born of the French countryside.* Our air, our sky, at once so clear and so soft, gave our artists their grace and refined their taste. The lark, national bird of France, alert and graceful, is the image of their genius. The lark abandons himself to the same flight, and the soaring of the stone lacework, like the wings of that bird, becomes iridescent in the silver-grey air.

Do you suppose, when the Druidic majesty of the great Cathedrals rising in the distance astonishes you, that they are the result of natural, fortuitous causes, such as their isolation in the country? You are mistaken. The soul of Gothic art is in this voluptuous declension of light and shadow which gives rhythm to the entire structure and makes it live. Here is a knowledge now lost, a deliberate ardor, controlled, patient, and strong, which our greedy and restless century is incapable of understanding. We must relive the past, return to principles in order to recover that strength. In those days a discerning taste ruled our land: we must become French once more! Initiation to Gothic beauty is initiation to the truth of our race, of our sky, of our land.

CHAPTER TWO

The French Countryside

I HAVE SAID that French Cathedrals are born of the French country-side.

Therefore none can understand them, none has the right to love them, unless he understands and loves that landscape.

Could you understand, could you love, Claude Lorrain or Corot if you did not respond to the landscape they understood, loved, and expressed?

So let us speak of Landscape before looking at Pictures. And let us seek this landscape in the provinces and small towns rather than in large cities, especially Paris. Science and industry have emptied and torn Paris. Let us look beyond. The provinces are still a refuge for taste, for style.

Between the past and the present what contrast!

For example a street: on one side the houses are still glorious examples of their time with noble lines, modest in their proportions, very beautiful, and with a power of seduction over me that is irresistible.

Then on the other side, just opposite, the street is being rebuilt in the "style of Babel." Quarried stones piled on top of each other without taste, without proportion.

How can the one take place beside the other? With the model before a person's eyes, how can he fail to see it? Only by refusing to see. The man who builds these hideous new houses must detest the beautiful old ones; he has marked them, condemned them, and will demolish them. O beautiful houses, be prepared for the wreckers!

When I speak of the Cathedrals as they are at present, I think of all our French villages; when I think of them in the past, I think of the genius of our French ancestors; at present and in the past I think of the beauty of the women of our country.

Nature is the earth and the sky; it is all men between that sky and that earth who suffer and who think; it is also the monuments those men have erected upon that earth and toward that sky.

Concerning all that, here are only a few unconnected notes. One could multiply them; it would be better to reduce them. They invite you to observe.

I · GOD DID NOT CREATE the sky in order that we should not look at it. Science is a veil: lift it and see!

Seek beauty.

It exists for the animals; it draws them. It determines their choice in the mating season. Creatures know that beauty is a sign, a guarantee, of goodness and health. But thinking beings, or those who believe they think, are now ignorant of what animals always know. We are formed for misfortune. An abominable education imposed on us from childhood obscures the light.

This factory smoke does not blacken the sky.

But in the foreground, the breath of industry overwhelms the view with an impenetrable, heavy fog that destroys perspectives and saddens our outlook.

Farther away, clouds dissolve into white plumes, joyous, formed of a thousand invisible currents.

So thought, achieving maturity, bursts into light while its origins remain unknown.

Clouds change, like conversations between agile and free minds.

They spread shadows here and there as a gardener, moving his sprinkler, pours refreshment to the right and left where it is needed.

Then all at once, clouds become white shoulders as smooth as satin.

Above them a silvery smudge makes the empty sky shine; beneath, on the wooded hills, are smooth expanses of light.

It is interesting to observe how clouds spread themselves out or draw themselves in, fragmenting and reassembling. So do human existences and loves.

I know this sky well. It is the one over Meudon. Every calm, clear day it fills the whole horizon with an equal splendor which is never exactly repeated.

The charming hillside becomes tinged with bronze: a wall of bronze, crowned.

Awhile ago the clouds were drawing white acanthus leaves in the sky, as definite as sculptures. Now there is a water color; and now drawings in India ink.

What happy lands are above the earth in the peace that is beyond all clouds.

Shall I honor this landscape by saying that it gives me an impression of Italy?

But the train rolling over its tracks cuts brusquely across this beloved country. I see the unwinding black back of a snake. It leaves white particles that are quickly effaced, emblems of busy times. Then the emphatic values of the day reappear, as if that tumultuous episode had not taken place.

This is a morning painted by Claude Lorrain, admirable in depth. Spring is here. I breathe in the delight of spring mornings. The rooster announces the day. An immense sigh is exhaled. Oh marvel! The earth in love! Fresh and happy landscape! There is nothing excessive in these proportions. Things do not compete with man in grandeur. But he, in this atmosphere that frees his spirit from petty matters, is able to conceive grandeur and to realize it.

The sky is full of slowly trailing clouds each more corpulent than the other. By their volume they govern and displace the light, always producing happy effects.

This site is rich in light thanks to harmoniously combined contrasts. The painter who would reproduce it would "flatten it out" unless he took those contrasts into account, a fault into which many a bad Impressionist has fallen.

Our gaze is drawn away, very far; the landscape is as if reflected in water and the majesty of Mount Valerien extends over this unreal, yet veritable, sheet of water.

I like to imagine that Mount Valerien is the Acropolis rendered in Corot's silvery grey tones. Ah Greece! I think of her at once whenever I feel on my lips this honey of admiration for beauty. Greece, that other sky inebriate with spring. And those two white tones over there on the hill would be the Parthenon.

The glory of this fruit tree in full flower in the foreground.

But the landscape's greatest beauty is given it by distance; that is, a superior beauty resides in the effects of depth.

And yet here is a charming exception: this whole hillside, including my house, is presented as a tapestry which does not recede. In the first distance a tree and the ramifications of its sparsely set branches; behind it the sky, flat and milky, except for the smiling tufts of lilac bushes; the landscape runs between these two distances, and the whole constitutes one great tapestry with no remote background.

This beautiful scene between the pilasters and arches of my museum, this deep, blurred perspective, shows far off the bridge at Sevres from where the course of the Seine returns toward me. The sky and objects in the background are grey. In the foreground an acacia tree is vigorously outlined.

This vestibule with its high arcades is restful, here outside vibrations penetrate by means of moving impressions. This type of architecture gives zest to the landscape, which is partitioned by the arches; graduations of the life and beauty of the landscape find frames in these high curves.

In going around the portico, one comes upon a faun perched high on its stand, offering the visitor the child in its arms. Near him a hedge, a tree. The tree fills the sky with pink-flowered branches.

Morning. Beneath this arcade, through the mist, I see the waking landscape. One can but vaguely discern the handsome bridge over the Seine. All of Saint-Cloud is lost in the milky atmosphere. No one would guess it was there who did not remember having seen it the evening before. Nothing seems real except the budding lilac plants. Their pale yellow hue becomes volatile in the soft light.

The clouds grow menacing. This aspect of things in anticipation was nevertheless delicious. And the plants rejoice. It is our miserable ignorance that keeps us from understanding and sharing in their joy and from being in harmony with nature!
Low clouds wander over the slope like sheep.

As a thought that becomes more precise, the slope is clarified. This is because the fog is falling away. The foreground darkens. But the admirable basin of the whole countryside blooms before my eyes, and the clouds, that were somber awhile ago, whiten.

Slender trees round themselves out. The ribs, a black armature of branches, are still visible among the young leaves. Trees of winter's end.

Now an infinite living poetry palpitates throughout the setting, tossing a scarf of joy over all, the round tufts of greenery, the houses, each one ideally placed, the damp, luminous sky and large airy clouds.

And still the hillside remains somber and slightly laden, with its boxed-in village and its observatory.

Versailles. This corner of the park is given a religious character by the beautiful vase in the center of the flower bed. That character is communicated to the trees which cluster around the circular path. And the vase itself owes its religious character to its antiquity.

A young woman was sitting on a bench. It seemed to me she was praying a Buddhist prayer.

Four young girls are coming along the road beside this meadow, color of springtime, four living images of happiness. They walk, light in the light air, as unconcerned as the grass and the flowers.

Meudon. The town is like a bouquet of flowers; the trees that seem to carry it at their summits do indeed support, limit, and contain it. How happy are these houses! Not modern. I see one behind the railroad, one of the humblest. It seems like a temple. These houses surrounded by greenery are like sheep in a park, passive amid blessings.

The landscape sleeps, overcome by a wholesome intoxication. A light wind; this fruit tree moves its head. Farther away, smoke from a small house rises like incense.
Nature's respiration enlarges and deepens the scene.
At intervals the rumble of a train recalls the passing of time through this eternity.

This eternity is not immobility. As the day develops, the aspects change. My meditation, but slightly interrupted, is resumed. I am faced by a scene which is not the one I had before me awhile ago and which I no longer recognize. The atmosphere is still grey, but a more luminous, a warmer, more passionate grey. The landscape wakens, still drunk, but with a new drunkenness that is purely sensual. Birds cut through the air like arrows, and the imperious and mistrustful sparrow that visits my window chirps insolently.

During this time, man also wakens to return to his work. The scraping sound of rakes reaches up to me.

The clouds are disturbed. The sky shines with a brighter light, too bright, announcing storm. Such disturbance is needed above us that the beneficent rain may fall over the fields. In the same way there must be pain so that the spirit may pour forth thought.

The atmosphere has relaxed. Pure vapors shine; the houses reflect light as though varnished. Smoke from the roofs floats in the uncertain air with no preferred direction. Then the plane of the hill in front of me darkens. All the interest lies beyond in those enchanted spaces where minds athirst for the marvelous send out the imagination as herald.

These perpetual changes of the French landscape offer the artist inexhaustible resources. It is necessary to have studied these changes in order fully to understand the art of the open air: in the Middle Ages, architecture and sculpture, in the 19th and 20th centuries, sculpture and painting.

By warming the plants, the sun has fulfilled its great function and lavished its blessing. But mist was needed; in the delicious grey light that mist produces, young shoots assert themselves and prepare for efforts. So the sun gave the order for mist.

This is an indispensable apprenticeship. Springtime is the season of youth, of timidity, of initiation. It is impossible to attain all at once to positive creative power, nor is it desirable that one should.

This landscape now at day's end, sprawls voluptuously beneath a sky of incomparable opulence. A Constantinople sky, pure blue with scattered clouds like rose-colored banners.

LE CHATELET-EN-BRIE · (*Wayside notes.*) What profound joy for a man of mature years to sum up his life by living what is admirable!

And all aspects of nature are admirable. It suffices to love in order to penetrate their secret. A single loving thought, the love of Nature, has repaid my whole life.

Three forces are struggling over this road: the wind, the clouds, and the sun. Wind and cloud are accumulations of jealousy and of violence directed against the sun, and I sense about the sun the ill-will of these two enemies.

On a pale ground of grey and blue silk, winter trees trace their embroidery. This is a state of affliction. And yet it is spring.

These trees at times darken like a wood, and at times they spread out, growing lighter. For whom is this spectacle offered? For no one. Or for a single passer-by along the road. The road itself is embellished with veils.

In the distance where trees that border the road draw together darkly, there is a wood. The slatelike clouds, greyish and wet, oblige us to return home, to trample the majesty of this road: triumphal way of pedestrians and herdsmen.

For a moment the sun withdrew from the road. But it returns, and I feel it breathing behind me. The road shines and is darkened according to the caprice of somber or brilliant clouds. This is a dappled day, brilliant as silver in the style of Louis XIV.

This village in sunlight level with the earth . . .

Now the sky is black, the earth pale and blond. The sun casts a white smile, and the trees and the ivy leaves tremble.

IN THE LOIRE COUNTRY · THE LOIRE, that aorta vein of our France; river of light and gently happy life! This morning is calm to the farthest horizons. All is in repose. Everywhere are the full effects of slowness and order. Well-being is visible on all sides through the colorful and balmy haze of fair weather.

Where, outside these regions, can one find this reassuring and comforting evenness of air and of light?

This subtle grey, this soft grey of the Loire beneath clouds, these grey rooftops of the city, this bridge, grey with old stones . . .

An irresolute sun capriciously lights the landscape.

This time I shall have seen no Cathedrals, but I have seen heaven itself pour down blue delight. Like acanthus leaves, clouds occupied the right, launching out in airy bounds like flights of Gothic angels.

Glorious day. The Loire, like steel, has a rippled design spreading across its whole breadth.

Oh, above all, the youthfulness of this sky! Its flower, its blue, and the sweet gaiety of its white inhabitants, the clouds!

All the joy of my youth returns to me.

This path that was coming towards us, bordered by shadows, turns back with its trees.

The Loire river like a scarf, like silver ribbons, grows faint in the underbrush of willow and poplar trees; greenery upon the first plane. In the meadow, what fortresses of poplars! Yellow moss harmoniously stains the greyish stones and trees.

Do not the houses of this vast plain remind one of cows that are pasturing? And those that form a long line are like oxen in single file, one after the other.

Plain of such beauty, of an order so simple, so noble! Here and there the greenery takes on a grave character. I find this same mixture and harmony among the people of this country, especially among its women, in their features and in the accent of their speech.

Three rows of linden trees. This is absolutely the triple nave of a Cathedral.

I was seated; I stand up: I had seen only half of this landscape; there was, besides, an immense emerald-colored meadow, some admirable trees, and this bridge over the slow river. The bridge has about it I know not what of an Egyptian temple dedicated to the moon.

Grandiose effects are produced by the simplification that fog brings to a landscape whose meadows and woods blend. These of nature's bas-reliefs are not pleasing to those who are charmed by precious materials—gold, silver, or jewels. These bas-reliefs are addressed to the spirit, to the superior understanding that perceives the geometry of forms. Geometry is divine. It speaks to our hearts because it is the general principle of things.

As one gazes for a long time at one's mistress before being separated from her, as one looks back to see her again and again, so I leave these beautiful landscapes as one tears oneself away from a beloved and loving heart. I leave them in full glory!

II · THE NEIGHBORHOOD OF MAGNY · *The church of Montjavoult.*

The portal of this church is rather like a Roman triumphal arch, but simpler, strongly in relief and squarely against the church wall.

What elegance! The Virgin occupies the center of the tympanum. Man has adored the germ in the oak; in Mary, the Incarnation and maternity, youth and fecundity, unite, and in her we adore the Mother and the Virgin at the same time.

Before this curving arch of Montjavoult, I understand the profound eloquence of the arc.

In the springing course of these circles over the coiled brackets, I see the satellite of a star. The columns on which the arch rests always present themselves so nobly! All of this is bordered by a molding as delicate as Greek tracery. Above is a decorative frieze of the dance of the plants with interweaving garlands.

Some black crows are perching on the molding.

This is not the Parthenon. It is the glory of French beauty.

In coming closer one makes out delicious details. The divine Renaissance knew no idolatry of the metropolis and made things as beautiful for peasants as for Kings.

I am the happy witness of these marvels. They are familiar to me. They accompany my thoughts, my admirations, my days.

And also, while I work outside, what impressions come to me from the chants inside the church! They are as sweet as the beautiful climate of this morning; they are an expression of peaceful lingering!

Ever the same harmonies, concerted by the centuries and as noble as the style that does not change but organizes the life of a people and prolongs it. The French race, still admirable by its men of thought, by its true artists, who shine with the same gleams as those of this sunset!

I love my country because I love its plants, its creatures, its glorious centuries. Shall it perish?

Shall the world perish as those great artists who speak to us now only in the language of stones?

At least so long as their life lasts, let us not be strangers to these marvelous stones in which the Occident flowered; they have all the delicate shades of mystery as well as the energy of reality.

The French temperament has realized perfection and has covered it with a veil of modesty. What the historian has not seen; the artist must be witness to.

The modesty of the French temperament is the modesty of the French landscape. A friend of art can be at home everywhere in France.

Morning, of the first Communion; cold frost, luminous mist.

There is no noise, no sound. One hears only oneself.

The road, the sky, these great belts of land resembling worn carpets or runners. The impalpable air reunites all in this absence of sun. Across this plain the wind slashes and wails. Its function is to purify whoever passes. Wind, cruel toward the afflicted.

This tree has received so many lashings from the wind that it bears profiles of misery. The day's sweetness is glimpsed through those openings.

The eddies, the repetitions, the gentle undulations recall the Atlantic Ocean. The land is like the wind, resigned.

One would guess that the ocean lay beyond: small fruit trees remind us of sailboats.

Nature labors in this infinite silence.

In the afternoon we walk up the path.

The church bell rings: it is for Vespers.

How comforting is this reminder of childhood and times past.

The road goes up until the sky is everywhere. At the top a carriage stands in glory. A fog of light, an immense dazzlement! Gentle agitation among the leaves. The cold sun also appears: today we are with that great healer, Nature.

The splendor of the Mont surges up before us. This is one Acropolis among thousands in France, art of the soul and of the spirit returning to Minerva.

The threshold of a house is always a triumphal arch that welcomes. What does it matter that this beautiful abode is unworthily inhabited!

MANTES · 39

40 · AUXERRE

LIMAY · 41

ETAMPES · 43

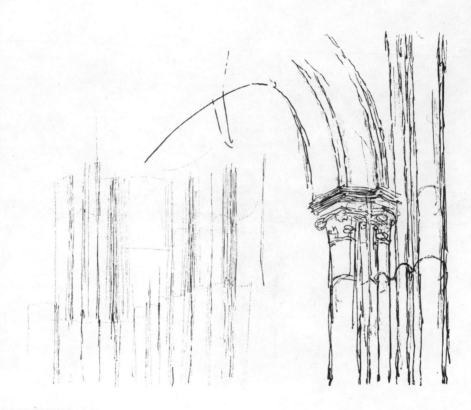

44 · CHAMPEAUX

STUDY · 45

46 · ETAMPES

Churches are milestones along the Roman roads of Christendom: Roman stations.

They are beautiful everywhere. When they were built, no one saw a difference between Paris and the provinces; and God, for the great artists, was the same in the capital and in a village. These great artists opened a sanctuary for all. Today we visit those sanctuaries, but we no longer feel that they are ours, although no one closes the door to us, and no one tells us, "Go away!" But chance or a whim decides us and we leave, not even knowing the happiness of the crows that nest in the belfry. Man has ceased to understand the Angelus: it means rest. The horse and the ox understand.

The Church of Cérans.

This church has the air of an enormous hen brooding over her chicks.

These ringed bell towers are a mixture of sculpture in the round and in bas-relief.

This one appears to detach itself from the rest. It overhangs the door and juts out in front of the stained-glass window which is behind and beyond. It models the ensemble, which appears like a beautiful morning. All the background of the building withdraws to give advantage to this tower, accompanied on the right and left by two simple buttresses. Thus it is like Christ at Mount Tabor between

Moses and Elijah. It has no definite form, but it has volume, and that is everything. One sees here how expressive are the masses seen from a distance by their plane and their situation. Beautiful relationships express nothing in particular but suggest a thousand things. This is true of a beautiful sculpture; even before we can exactly distinguish it, it has already moved us.

The ribs of the ceiling are like the branches of trees.

These leaves catch their balance like birds that catch on to the nest.

In this leaf that springs up is the same spirit that made the heroes and martyrs.

How these profiles carry! How proud they seem to me from where I stand beneath them! They make a roof against the sky. How rich these blacks are in this broad open daylight; they are alternated just as the surfaces are. Here one feels a Roman lineage.

The sense of proportion in Gothic ornamentation continues to be felt to the time of Louis XIV, inclusively.

In the country, red upon an even ground, the winter sunset glistens against the mildew of bared trees.

Oh, divine gift of being engrossed to a certain degree in this great drama, of being able to understand and take part in it!

III · *Beaugency*.

With my elbows on the window sill of my hotel room, I gaze far and wide over the world and, like God the Father, I judge it.

I see the passing of a light cart drawn by a donkey. In the cart a whole little family, the mother, still youthful, the daughters and sons, and the father growing old—Saint Joseph. All are wearing their best clothes, and I admire their elegance. Indeed all the fine clothes of this little family, and of all who pass to and fro about the cart, appear elegant to me. These are for the most part blouses, loose over-garments whose folds reveal the body and the trade of those who wear them.

What a soft neutral haze is diffused over this small country, over the trees and houses, over the garments, and over the harmonious movements of men and of animals! Young girls pass, triumphant, the pride of the land and of the race.

With benevolence I exercise my functions as judge; as many as come, I pass to the right. Thus as many as come are saved. But here are people who never guess how fortunate they are. For, without my interference, are they not happy indeed? They are peaceful, and their life flows away in half silence. They are like this spring season, still pale and close to winter, but having sun and warmth within.

This folk is very gentle, completely estranged from the severe epoch in which their Romanesque Cathedral was born. And yet, this population, excommunicated by the pharmacists and scholars, has in general retained a taste for prayer. It is to the church that the little family is going in their small cart. As they enter they will gaze respectfully at the awesome perspectives and guess that heaven is their goal.

This does not hinder the wife from seeing her husband as a master, a god. The children, among whom there will be young artisans, gaze with all their eyes and all their intelligence: they understand! Because they are simple, they assimilate without difficulty the part of this mystery that is destined for them. Because the church is a work of art derived from nature it is accessible to simple and true minds. In any case, old Saint Joseph, the father, has left for the cabaret. He holds forth. (I can hear no one else.) He talks nonsense; he lords it, proud of his grown daughters. Soon his children and his wife join him. One feels that the reunited family is all vibrant with innocent pride and joy.

It is Easter.

A little French girl seen at church:

A lily-of-the-valley in flower wearing a new dress . . . Sensual pleasure is as yet a stranger to these adolescent lines. What modest grace! If this young girl knew how to look and to see, she would recognize her portrait in all the portals of our Gothic churches, for she is the incarnation of our style, of our art, of our France.

From my place behind her, I saw only the general outline of her person and the downy rose of her cheek, half child, half woman. But she lifts her head, turns away for an instant from her small book, and the profile of a young angel appears. Here in all her charm is the young girl of the French provinces: simplicity, integrity, tenderness, intelligence, and that smiling calm of true innocence which is transmitted like a sweet contagion and pours peace into the most troubled hearts.

Modesty and Moderation are the principal qualities of French womanhood. Our young girls (far from Paris) wear those two words clearly inscribed on their foreheads, and the modern spirit by miracle has not yet been able to rub them away. On the banks of the Loire particularly, one often recognizes admirable feminine examples of the original freshness of the race. Therefore let nothing be changed in the education of our women; they are indeed fine as they are. Even the most beautiful Venus of antiquity was less beautiful. Let nothing be removed. The masterpiece is still of our day. But alas! Change will come about in spite of us, and it has already begun.

The architecture of our Cathedrals was necessary to the beauty of these women as an imposing and well-proportioned frame. One no longer realizes this and yet it is certain. In the shadow of the church, an atmosphere gathers where one feels the serious palpitating thought of studious men, where music gives rhythm to the fair hours of the day and the great days of the year, where poetry is not wanting nor heroes nor the faithful, where a woman feels in her soul and in her flesh that she is respected by all; that is where the one who will be our living Victory* could be born and nurtured.

What will be left tomorrow of all that? What remains even now? It is a miracle that there should still exist young girls like the one I admired in the church of Beaugency. They come to us out of the past; we may meet a few of them for a while longer, at least in the less "civilized" regions of the provinces.

But it seems to me that from this day forward they share the fate of those Cathedrals for which their forebears served as models: they are no longer in style.

What a pity that the greater number of our girls from the provinces should go to Paris. What a hideous waste of beauty that monster makes! It is the glory of France, the river of our life, of our energy, that is being exhausted.

There are still the provinces, I very often say to myself for consolation.

In one gesture these girls bring us all grace and all power. Their

* *Translator's note:* The Victory of France, which would rival the Victory of Samothrace.

presence illumines our existence. And their modesty is proportionate to their power. The benedictions of the city and of the world are its young women. Bearers of life, sensitive forms of hope and of joy, substance of all masterpieces, so close they are to Nature. Their movements never sin against divine geometry. They restore the soul of those who understand them. *Virgin*: what a wondrous word. *Mother*: tenderness that equals beauty. As for me, the potter, happy to turn in the image of their gracious forms vases that give the illusion of their beauty, countless times a day my thought goes out to them. Not only do they have charm, they have kindness also, and they are sometimes slandered, as happens also to genius.

What a school the street is! Here gestures are natural, garments fall easily. The bearing of young women going to church is without false modesty, the torso straight, the step firm in the peaceful street of a small town. These are not women of fashion, not those in whose transparent flesh, perfumed by the most precious scents, life would fear to show itself, where the soul hides. I speak of beings who are simple, true, sound, and very much alive, of women predestined for joy and for sacrifice, whom we love and cause to suffer.

In a moment of anger, when we have abused their patience, lightning flashes from them, and prophetic voices whose accent astonishes us are engraved on our memory to rise suddenly when we need to be recalled to duty.

This child of our race, seated on the steps of the portal, this peasant yet delicate figure, will give in the second generation fruits of very great beauty. How white this page is still! What peace!

Woman is the true Holy Grail and she is never more beautiful than kneeling; the Gothics thought of this. A church from the outside is shaped like a woman on her knees.

The provinces are still full of admirable reserves of moral riches. There one constantly finds that depth of feeling which is in our blood as it has been transmitted to us by our ancestors. From this is inexhaustively recruited the admirable abnegation of the sailor, of the soldier, of the aviator. This marvelous courage makes us doubt the power of evil! Therein one still finds the elements of a true humanity.

IV · THE TIME of the rationalizers has returned. As always they babble, they hold forth learnedly; they will agree only to what they can understand. They discant on the art of the Middle Ages and raise a thousand questions, almost all of which they leave without resolution; for each one that they do not abandon, they propose several systems.

But, reasoners, a simple companion of yore did not resort to so much ceremony, he found right away in himself and in nature, the truth you seek in libraries! Their truth was Reims, it was Soissons, it was Chartres, it was those sublime Rocks of all our great cities: that truth was the very genius of France.

Those companions of long ago had a soul, the soul that architecture needed to feel *behind it*, to bring its principles to the supreme expression of nuances.

Compared with you, doctors, I am willing to admit that they may have been children, those artisans and workmen: only, they were children in the School of Truth. And are you?

Ah, those workmen! That we should not even know how to pronounce the names of those humble and sublime men who had such knowledge!

Often I dream that I see them, that I follow them from city to city, those pilgrims of Work, consumed by the passion to create. With them I visit the Mother, who assembles those Companions of the Tour of France. We gather at one table for lunch. We are young and vigorous. Each tells what he knows. The appreciations of these seers, the discussions between them concerning beautiful things, their science and their thought in which the colossus that is coming into being is reflected. They work at Reims. They have seen Saint-Denis, Chartres, Noyons, Amiens. And several of them have worked at one and the other. They have in their gaze and in their soul all that glory. Titans!

Yet these are very simple men, not unlike the brothers of those men and young girls from the provinces whose lives we were considering a while ago. But the great thought of their time is in them and, to realize that, these men are in constant relationship with nature; and they are strong and sound. They have the sobriety, constancy, and energy of great noble animals who keep their natural functions in working order. Over these powerful organisms the soul hovered, ceaselessly retempering it that it might not be lost in the regions of pride and vain illusions. Thus those little children were able to conceive, and to realize their conceptions, those robust companions.

How I should love to sit at table with such stone carvers.

V · WHY did they build these colossal bulwarks, the Cathedrals?

It was to deposit—in safety as they believed—the imperceptible egg, that seed which requires so much patience, so much care: TASTE, that atom of pure blood which the centuries have transmitted to us, and which, in our turn, we should transmit.

All these proud equilibriums, all these accumulations of stone glorified by genius, that rise to the extreme limit where human pride would lose contact with life, with the species, and would totter in the void, all such is but the tabernacle. Or rather—for this shrine is living!—it is the Sphinx, guardian of the Secret.

The secret is virtually lost, since today only a few can reply to the Sphinx crouching on all sides of our French cities.

We should know how to respond to the Gothic sphinx if nature herself had not become for us an incomprehensible sphinx.

In the Cathedral there is all the simple beauty of the menhir, which foretells it.

Incontestably, Romanesque and Gothic blocks recall, in larger size, the Druidic stones.

So do great trees have their part in the creation of Cathedrals. As much as old stones whose accumulation constitutes the Cathedrals, I love the mighty trees; between trees and stones I see a kinship. Were not the enormous logs that upheld the Gallic huts prototypes of buttresses, or buttresses themselves?

In buttresses there is, moreover, a primitive and charming reminder of a Roman dwelling.

Roman art and the barbaric buttress are in the Cathedral.

And these hands supported the vaults, these extending tendons!

Cyclopean walls are made gay by ever decorative vegetation. In this way Gothic genius assembled and steadily piled up stones, from the foundations. And at the very height it adjusted flowerlets, hooks, and thorns in imitation of climbing vegetation.

All the lines are lines of victory. They rise superbly to the limit of height, carried there by the logical development of the building as a whole.

This is the result that schools always try for without success, because schools invent rules that are not ratified by nature. Nature refuses to be grafted onto our dreams. It remains faithful to its own laws that never deceive; as the sea has its limits, movements have their equilibrium. The Gothics invented nothing. Inventions are blasphemies.

Economy of effects. Here are columns and colonettes that mount to the ceiling in one straight plane. To be effective, they ask no more than the strong salient capitals. We find this principle repeated in the wall of the Theater at Orange, at two-thirds of whose height, thick and highly protruding stones give the broad surface its powerful beauty.

In the background, at the summit of the high naves, a ray of light filters and spreads to illumine the whole, playing at different levels. Overhead in this sky of stone, one seems to see a storm cloud.

The violet gleams from the stained glass tinge the apse with tones from an Impressionist palette.

Woman, according to the Book of Genesis, was created after man; grace follows strength.

Gothic art is always darker; its forms are more closely woven than those of the Renaissance. The Renaissance spreads out its forms, dissolving them in the incomparable grace which is its hallmark and in the softness which is its expression. It conserves the black furrows at wide intervals: this is the Attic quality in French art. Its generally blond tone finds in those very rare blacks the accent, the spring, that sets that blond tone in value. I know nothing so entrancing. In the 13th, 14th, and 15th centuries, a more fervent power was expressed with more energy. The Renaissance tempered the fervor of love.

Declension from the Gothic to the Renaissance style of the 16th century, you forced me to study light. I strove to understand your motives, your thousands of ribs, and to put certain of your riches into my works.

It is indeed Taste, the sense of what is appropriate, the sense of relationships, that makes the unity of the Cathedral. Taste presides over the placement of belfries, of portals, of all the members of this great Living Being, all of whose members are developed in the round, which alone can nourish and sustain the lines, can harmonize with images, and express itself despite distance and by means of distance.

Writers on art also defend taste, recommending proportion and clarity. I am not quite sure that by the same words we understand the same things. It is of the clarity and of the taste of effects that I speak. Taste is the adaptation of human will and human forces to the will and forces of nature.

Photographs of monuments are mute for me. They do not move me; they allow me to see nothing. Because they do not properly reproduce the planes, photographs are for me always of an unendurable dryness and hardness. The lens of the camera, like the eye, sees in low relief. Whereas, looking at these stones, I feel them! My gaze touches them everywhere as I move about to see from all sides how they soar in every direction under the heavens and from all sides I search out their secret.

Strength is repugnant to the weak. Not understanding it, they do not desire it.

The Cathedral was achieved slowly and passionately. The Romans brought it their might, their logic, their serenity. The Barbarians brought it their naïve grace, their love of life, their dreams, their imagination. From this collaboration, which came without premeditated design, the work germinated, modeled by time and place.

The Cathedral is the image of French genius. It did not come about by fits and starts nor in obedience to pride. It rose to expression over a succession of centuries.

And this expression throughout the country varies with each province, and each fraction of province, just enough for history to record the chain that links together all the pearls of this monumental necklace of France.

Our atmosphere, the air of our country, at once so sharp and so shrouded in mists, guided our Gothic and Renaissance artists. Their art is as soft as the light of day.

The Greeks knew no other way for making their masterpieces.

By the precision of its resolve, by its knowledge of the declension of light, the Gothic-Renaissance joins, and has no need to envy, Greek art.

Ah Renan, you left Brittany to prostrate yourself before the Parthenon. A sculptor raised by the Greeks comes from the Parthenon and goes to Chartres to adore the Cathedral.

We have lost at once the sense of our race and of our religion. Gothic art is the conscious, tangible soul of France; it is the religion of the French atmosphere. We are not unbelieving; we are only unfaithful.

In the majesty with which the Cathedral is shrouded as by an immense cloak, the noises of daily life—the footfalls, the sound of rolling wheels, of a door that closes—all resound. Solitude regulates those sounds according to a harmonious sense of proportions.

The outlines fill and become decorative at this distance. It is the buttresses that give this shapely sweep. The majestic train of the apse makes a royal cloak.

And the flying buttresses in profile are swallows in flight, also sometimes the swinging of thuribles.

These grave artists of the 12th century, of the 13th, and of the Renaissance, up to the end of the 18th century, worked with a joy that is everywhere felt in their work. Great poets, they gave us their thought, that is to say, their flesh and their blood.

For them art was one of the wings of love, and religion was the other. Art and religion give humanity all the certainties it needs to live by and which are unknown to epochs dimmed by indifference, that moral fog.

And how they loved life! In life they sought their art, its principles and its consequences, with that singleness of thought which makes the unity of great destinies. Did they not dress their wives with the same taste as their works? And has not feminine elegance its part in the lace of the pinnacles and in the folds of the small columns?

These white columns, nervures, windows, vertical transoms, these trefoils suggest the sun's natural light coming through leaves.

Gothic moldings are sometimes inspired by a tempest. They are like the sea in movement.

The molding, that thread which runs in horizontal or vertical sense, is also in nature: it is the course of the sap. Leaves and flowers were reserved for ornaments.

The console, so accentuated by the Renaissance, is Gothic in its general form, in its outline. Looking at this portal, with its rows of saints whose bent heads and whose feet rest upon accessories, I see the console which is the generating line of the whole edifice.
That line reigned to the time of Louis XVI.

The tympanum was first of all given to sacred history, the Bible and the Gospel: creation, the prophets, Christ the judge, the coronation of the Virgin, etc.
Later, it became a pure decoration; not a simple decoration. Pleasing in itself, it unrolls and returns in a foliated scroll. This is the Renaissance, another movement, a declension of the same thought.
And nevertheless this decoration is admirable because of its re-

straint. Proportions are respected. Life is expressed in its static manifestation.

The human body is dramatic in itself. It is also a standard of harmony. How is it possible that there are sculptors who give us an inexpressive, indifferent Christ Crucified? Simply as a human being, the Crucified would be singularly moving. Represented by an artist's chisel, Christ in death becomes more living than a live man.

Sometimes the genius of certain races accentuates expression to the point of producing a shiver of terror. I recall a Christ in a church on the Rue Haute in Brussels: this is not the Eucharistic victim of love; nothing is left but suffering. That Christ is Spanish.

What do breaks matter! Draw from the mutilated figures; the planes will still be there. (An artist understands what I mean.) If the planes are right, the break proves it. Tirelessly I will repeat: the plane is all. An eye made with a nail has divine gradations of light and of thought if the plane is true; an eye chiseled by the most perfected tools, and even most lovingly, is inexpressive if the plane is false. What use would the delicious fine lines of her mouth or of her profound gaze be to the Mona Lisa if the planes of her face were not all in place?

Repairs dry and become dark very quickly: artificial aging. Do they believe they fool us? They darken in vain; they remain dated, being hard and flabby at the same time.

Mellow grey and soft; such softness is a quality of times past, a quality of style.

An art that has life does not restore works of the past, it continues them.

Here is a palace to which a true artist, an artist of former times, has made a small addition: a charming motif which does not disturb the columns that are connected with each other. Between two of them is the modest little Renaissance ornament which, thanks to its grace, is forgiven the audacity of being placed there. With what suppleness and wealth of invention it has "turned" to produce the *ensuing style,* while it disturbs nothing in the light of the preceding style! This is what it means to follow the primary idea while directing it toward another plane which does not trouble the general and essential order: this is Taste.

Originality, if this word may be taken in an affirmative sense, does not consist in forging new words deprived of the beautiful characteristics of experience, but in a fine usage of old words. Old words are adequate for all. They are sufficient for genius.

Senlis: purity of faith, purity of taste.

Those flowers that rise to the vaults! The arc that launches out from the capital without being detached from it! What supreme art in a single stroke! To accomplish that without meagerness required all the genius of those incomparable artists.

The curves of the vault running between the ogival ribs form flat bands resembling ribbons. The black shadow is behind. Between these ribbons, the rib is formed by a type of modeling in lower relief, as was necessary. The Renaissance style, by slightly attenuating the Gothic modeling in the round, creates charming Greek effects.

How comforting is the spectacle of a small provincial town before six o'clock in the morning, for example *Blois*. Great haste toward work in the factories; the houses are clean and modest with their shutters closed; and the beautiful strong bridge which, thanks to the effect of its highly curved back, is like a road in the midst of the sky.

Behind a curtain of houses, a massive Romanesque bell tower comes into view, admirable in power. The pretty little faces of the time of Louis XV—of which I am reminded here—saw this handsome stone belfry which springs like a flower from a garden. But already they found it hideous.

I turn back toward the bridge over which carriages valiantly make the ascent at regular intervals, their profiles outlined against the sky, and I see, in this mounting and descending, an image of life.

Clarity in constraint: Blois.

In its castle and in its church, Blois has been stricken by our time. Ah, the money-changers have entered the temple!

Lost harmonies. The new stained-glass windows are strangers to the words that are sung in this church. The relation between windows and words was nevertheless intimate originally. The soul of things is betrayed by caricature.

There is a street in Blois so graceful that, seeing it foreshortened from a certain point, one has the impression of a monument. Here is the discrete grace, caressing to the eyes and the heart of an artist, that I have tasted in so many provincial towns. In these perspectives one finds the very charm of a monument which constitutes the glory of the small town.

Leaving the church, I stop again to look at the façades. Fragmented chants reach me at intervals like gusts of air from above. Meantime I study the stones and wood of the door: Adam and all his daughters, goddesses of their time, charming in the modesty of their attitudes.

The usefulness of a "subject" is to focus the mind and to *save it from dispersion*. But the true importance is beyond that. Our contemporaries barely suspect this "beyond." They claim the right to *understand.* To understand what? What the artist wanted to say. But the subject does not inform us of the artist's intentions. *That must be sought for in the execution.* Take for example a bas-relief; by the opposition of its planes, the artist has created beautiful shadows from which there looms a head, the neck of a nymph, or her knees: all is of an infinite grace. That grace is what is important to *understand.* As for knowing whether the figures represent summer, autumn, etc., all such is secondary. There are even compositions whose subject eludes notice: this hidden figure holding a book, what does it signify? Mystery. And ornament? Isn't ornament the utilization of light and shadow without a subject? There is a more precious mystery to be penetrated, that is the mystery of art, of beauty. For that our public has small concern, preferring dry lines to the most masterly modeling, provided the anecdote can be made out. Isn't that true also of religion?

I perceive a form: it is a figurine. I distinguish nothing clearly; but by the shadow, by the light which separates darkness from day, by that which I do not see, by the well-poised mass which my eye weighs, I feel, and thus see, a masterpiece. Neither the light nor the mass of shadow are important; it is the modeling, it is the equilibrium that makes itself felt. When a figure is true in its contrasts, one feels the equilibrium, and if the equilibrium is good, one senses the possibility of movement, of life. And my spirit knows a sense of plenitude: this belongs to the Antique! I recognize its divine harmony. That is what had to be *understood*.

Like beauty, consciousness makes itself felt from afar. Take that magisterial figure. It dominates the visitors who pass; it stops those who understand it. What expression in this face! As in many Roman busts, here it is the critical period of life that the artist has rendered in all its moving verity. Years have passed during which this figure has been beautiful. It is still of lofty bearing, just as it is, on its knees, and before God. What atmosphere surrounds it! How much at rest in kneeling throughout three centuries! And how this figure lives in its repose thanks to the perfection of the modeling.

Modeling by planes is the whole life of architecture and of sculpture. It is the soul of stones touched by the artist. It is also the relation between small proportions, above all in depth. An unmodeled or badly modeled detail is an insolent stupidity. All is flat in our stones that are carved today; they are without life.

Saint-Cloud: Here the beauty of the flowers, however ill arranged, consoles us for the ancient architectural splendors that have disappeared.

Magnificent avenue of a palace that is no more.

I saw that palace when I was young. It seems to me this destruction furrows time, inflicting upon it an incommensurable recession.

The palace was an admirable example of order and harmony.

In the gardens I admire the *Apollo*. What majesty. The openings, like those formed by the handles of a vase, give the torso precious lightness. What grace is in this mass. The three-quarters view and the back show that this figure is entirely in the taste of Michelangelo.

The architect responsible for Saint-Cloud had the happy idea of placing there beautiful casts. I was so fearful of finding—as elsewhere—horrible copies!

It is when they are seen from below that these ancient figures attain their full beauty. Look for instance at the Victory of Samothrace. She soars, and *moral* wings, when there are no real ones, always accompany and envelop her.

What grace in this *Genius of Eternal Repose!* To think that the misunderstood ancient art should have brought forth a whole numberless school, the School that caricatures the Antique! These "masters" have looked at all they thought they saw, at the Antique and the Gothic as well as at nature, with murderous eyes. This *Genius of Eternal Repose* seen from a distance is greater than the *Apollo*, greater than Michelangelo.

It is remarkable with what ease Greek art can get along without the Greek light. But wherever that art is exiled, it longs for the gentle clarity spoken of by Homer.

In the region of *Tours* there is a little church* which has not been repaired or, at least, not wholly. For the chancel, which was Romanesque, an engineer, no doubt from a well-known sanitation department, was consulted; he did his job.

But in the nave are marvelous modelings, delicate pillars, great and so-fresh ribs that are divided into several more delicate ribs.

Thus each excursion holds surprises for my admiration. Sometimes it seems that beauty—dare I say it?—tricks me. I have just had that experience once again at Melun.

In a church corner, I had admired some little sculptured marvels, lovingly added as second thought, the flowers of a Renaissance bouquet. Impatient to see them again, I returned to the church this morning: they were changed. My still-enchanted memory of the splendors of yesterday is today disappointed. My "masterpieces" are mediocre! But wait! A few minutes of attention and here are other beauties worthy of those of yesterday. Other things, drowned in shadow before, show themselves now giving impressions that are as

* Saint-Symphorien.

charming as the first. The privilege of sculpture in the round, of that strong projection, is to give the sweetness of the half-tone, or let us say, rather, of chiaroscuro. Still, if I had brought a friend there with me, announcing these wonders to him, it seems to me that I should have been abashed at first for my masterpieces; and then the retreat would have been changed into victory. The impression would have been different from the one I had announced, but equally beautiful. A work at once *new* and *the same*.

Everywhere there are beautiful remains, enough still to console several generations of artists.

Study these magnificent fragments and, if you wish to understand, go to see them at different hours of the day. These works made in the open air change their beauty as the hours change, and their variation is upon a constant theme. Evening will reveal to you what morning did not allow you to see.

These works are transformed as beautiful feminine faces are in which the same soul, that cannot say all the first time, continues to speak manifesting itself at different hours of the day with so many nuances!

In front of the Cathedrals I feel uplifted, transported by a sense of Justice. Plastic soundness is the image and correspondence of moral justice.

I open the door. What order! The idea of perfection is impressed upon my mind. What eternal foundations! And that architectural virtue which I love so much, that breadth so lacking in our epoch! Solidity and depth that survive the centuries! With passion I breathe this power. This is the amplitude of the Temple of Paestum, sturdy in the landscape like a bull on the plain or like a Greek phalanx; that is the Antique breadth. In Gothic art it grows slender and soaring.

At the other end of the church the Holy of Holies is in darkness; it forms a great line of separation that soars to the apex, lifting itself to the point where power falls back to rest upon the other capital.

Below, that line separates the chancel from the congregation, like the curtain of a venerable theater where gestures and words are ancient and produced amid ancient gloom, where only the gold of a hanging lamp glimmers.

My spirit mounts following that line and falls back with it, to rise again. The beating of my heart also follows that line, then takes up the rhythm of the blind arcades that palpitate up high and far away.

A large silence in which one feels the sages deliberating within themselves.

The priest enters; repose, then the chants.

Women make the church fragrant by their beauty.

The congregation, in confused voices, humbly expresses love and adoration for Justice. Above is the organ coiling in and out like serpentine lightning. And the murmur of human voices *binds* the organ's deep chant.

Rembrandt, whom you admire in the 17th century, of whom you would make a classic, is intensely Gothic. Rembrandt's genius is also life in shadow.

But take care to notice that shadow does not exist in itself. It is a garment that attaches to the form. If the form is good, the shadow, which is its manifestation, will be expressive. Give me beautiful forms, and I shall have beautiful shadows. That which makes the variety of styles is the declension of those same shadows with different details. Also there is perfect unity in French art, from the Romanesque to our day—and to ours exclusively. We have denied ourselves by refusing our love to the marvels of our past, and that denial is suicide.

VI · How in good faith, could anyone excuse or explain the modern crime, the abandonment of the Cathedrals? Still worse: their murder and parody!

We are the unconscious executioners of our own condemnation. Destiny withdraws from us these great titles to glory because we no longer deserve them, and, to consummate our shame, it charges us with carrying out our own punishment.

Is it man who has diminished? Is it the Divinity? How could it be that God would require a ridiculous tribute from us now, after such spendid sacrifices?

If we have grown infirm, since when dates our infirmity?

Are we truly reduced to such feebleness that, with no effort to hold it back, we should allow the great mystic bird to fly away?

The Cathedrals ought to give us so much pride! They have engendered the force whose last manifestations still enlivens us. Have you no more the desire for health? Do you no longer even understand what it is?

The Cathedrals are France. As I contemplate them I feel our ancestry mounting and descending in me as if by another Jacob's ladder.

Oh what a shame to see vast residences built at great expense for comfort and luxury, but which are hideously sumptuous, while our true motives for glory perish!

Is it perhaps necessary for suns to set?

We live very close to many beautiful things but most of us do not see them. And they persuade and preserve so few minds among those who see them.

Our ignorance of masterpieces is the forgetting of our truth. As beauty penetrates sight, it awakens the heart to love, and without love nothing has value.

But love is no longer taught.

If the understanding of beauty were a matter of education or of instruction, how could we be deprived of it, we moderns, who are privileged among all? Have we not in our museums Egypt, Assyria, India, Persia, Greece, and Rome? And have we not on our own soil vestiges of Gothic and Romanesque art, as well as those charming marvels, our old houses, still beautifully proportioned through the First Empire, and so severely elegant in their period style with an eloquent grace, even to its reserve, which is sometimes inscribed in a simple band without moldings?

We have all that, and our architects put up the buildings that you know. While in statuary, casting from life, that cancerous sore of art, prospers!

Ah Proportion, synthesis of the arts, perfection that cannot be grasped! The sense of your truth penetrates us slowly with a sort of salutary terror which purifies and ennobles us. But where are you now? Artists seem to have lost even the notion of your existence since they renounced building God's temple, since they undertook to raise the temple of human vanity. And for this new temple they want more precious materials, lavished with more ornaments than were ever seen before. But vanity confesses the spiritual poverty of the vain. There are too many moldings in our palaces. Proportion is becoming to man's dwelling, as it is to himself.

Are not the Jews proud of their Bible, the Protestants of their morality, the Mussulmen of their Mosque? Do not all protect these witnesses of their faith and of their history!

We lack that fidelity, we who do not defend our Cathedrals.

And what should we defend in them? Our ignorance prevents us from seeing that they are admirable, and why, and how. Priests ask for new churches from the architects of our *music halls* and order their statues of saints from merchants.

What has become of the bleeding heart of those crowds of old that bequeathed to us these poignant testimonies of their sorrow and their genius? These are the true relics. What has become of the Christian Parthenon? Younger than the other, it is more decrepit.

Are we then more barbarous than the Arabs? They respect monuments from the past. What they do by indifference, could you not do by duty, inasmuch as Gothic monuments have been entrusted to you? One dare not ask: could you not do it for love and for your joy?

I wish to tell you what treasures you disdain.

They belong to all; each Frenchman has his part ownership, as in the depth of his soul he has his share of moral life.

To bring our people to the Cathedral is to lead them home, to their dwelling, to the citadel of their power. The country cannot perish so long as the Cathedrals endure. They are our Muses. They are our Mothers.

Come and see your own, see what is being taken from you. There still remain magnificent ruins.

Lost faith, beauty forgotten.

Europe, like an old, weary Titan, changes its stance and consequently its equilibrium. Will it be able to adapt to new conditions, or will it lose, rather than change, its equilibrium? No one knows. It is certain that if modern man lacks taste, he does not lack grandeur and courage. Witness the aviators.

The memory that one carries from the Cathedrals imposes silence, a fertile silence in which the soul knows its great well-being, the feast of thought. One meditates upon the counsel that Nature has just given us by means of art. One searches for the law.

It cannot be exactly defined. Measure, a certain order, there is the law. And it is also taste, wisdom, reason, fitness. It is immortality as well as the link which unites century to century, man with the men of his race and from different countries and which unites our spirit with Nature.

80 · STUDY

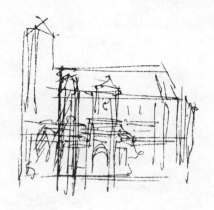

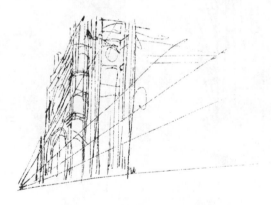

82 · TONNERRE

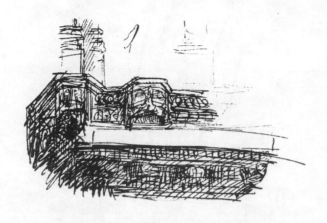

84 · DIJON

STUDY · 85

86 · USSÉ

But in this concert of the centuries, the 19th as art is a discordant note; a halt in their progression. Will it count in future judgment? Flat, even to the character of individuals, this century has ignored depth, one of the three measures. It has misunderstood one of the three parts of geometry.

You shall see what beautiful city halls will be built in the provinces when there will be no more Louis XVI castles where municipal offices may be lodged.

In great works of the past one does not always understand at once the sequence of opposing planes. But one must manage to take that in, because it is from such opposition that equilibrium and "tournure"* result. Now this secret is unknown to the architects who have undertaken to restore the Cathedrals while adding thereto the vices of our epoch. Also they always tend to overload the structure, to weary it. They miss the effect they strive for because they do not know the requirements of equilibrium.

The blessed shadow of the Cathedral continues to stretch over me for a long while after I have crossed its threshold; it accompanies me in life. I see again the great lines of its architecture, certain details of

* *Translator's note:* Shape.

its sculpture, such a figure that in isolation makes a complete unit, a world apart, an image of the whole. Thus the smallest insect, because it accords with general laws, offers us a representation, abridged yet total, of the universe.

VII · CIRCUMSTANCES will not prevail against Spirit and against Law.

The sense of beauty is necessary and imperishable. I am convinced of this by feeling so vividly within myself the ability to admire. This ability all men have. It may slumber, but it will awake.

Neither have I always understood the whole truth. What gratitude I owe to the forces that have revealed it to me! Today, on this spring morning whose atmosphere is in flower, my memories escort me. I rejoin my past. I think of the long and delicious studies that have given me a taste for life and taught me its secret.

Whence comes this favor?

First from my long walks through the forest where I discovered the sky, the sky that formerly I believed I had seen every day, until one day I did see it.

And then also from the model; the living model without speaking to me brought about the birth of my enthusiasm, made patience possible, gave me the joy of understanding this flower of flowers, the human flower. Since then my admiration has always broadened and heightened. My faculty of observation has been sharpened, thanks to rare and ardent affections and thanks to springtimes like this one in which the earth sends its flowering soul to the surface to dazzle and enchant us.

What delight for me to have a profession that allows me to declare my love for Nature. Oh! this model, this temple of life, of which the art of sculpture may reproduce the most tender modulations, the most delicate lines which at first one might believe most deceptive, whose least fragment is already the masterpiece as a whole. And this face, where the divine soul, strength, freshness, and grace are joined as in their favorite abode and in the seat of our admirations!

Behold the honey I have amassed in my heart. I live in perpetual gratitude toward God and toward his admirable creatures, his eloquent emissaries.

Others would enjoy this same happiness. And I am well aware that already others do at this very moment, as in all centuries, adore beauty with me.

Beauty will not perish.

May I be allowed to dwell for a moment on the joys given me by masterpieces and by my own works? Therein may lie an example.

Leaning from the window of my hermitage at Meudon, I bathe my brow in the morning dew. All somber thoughts withdraw, I yield to the sweetness of this beautiful springtime hour. I know that my sculptured folk await me to be seen and to work with me.

But I shall stop first at my little museum where beautiful works of all epochs are gathered. Many of my own sculptures are there, and they are recognizable even though by instinct I am always drawn toward Tradition. *Originality* is an empty word. A word of the garrulous and the ignorant: It has lost many students and many artists. It is impossible for us sculptors to have originality. We are copyists. The Gothics had so much fecundity only because they copied nature. We are men of study.

Study is a very kind sister who never leaves you. She keeps you company even when you do not invite her to join your work. And how little is necessary to direct her attention and make her useful!

Today I am held by this little museum that I ordinarily and so ungratefully abandon, being assured that matters of first importance call me elsewhere. The museum is in a delicious semidarkness which the haze of beautiful weather has penetrated. My gaze alights on objects that have a familiar enchantment for me. These plasters, these marbles, hold little conversations with me, reminding me of my pilgrimages to all the Cathedrals of France. Enchantment! I hear vague murmurs, then more distinct words and, finally, dominating strophes. The souls of the Masters teach and correct my soul.

Despite the diversity of epochs, everything here proceeds according to the same law of harmony. Nearly all these works are masterpieces, which is to say that all these sculptures are born complete. It is in this respect that they seem to me, and they are, similar to one another. No, not one is original. The glorious praise inherent in these recurrent foliated scrolls has all the fullness of powerful hymns, whose effect is also the result of repetition.

The nerve that holds this leaf as it climbs vigorously, is the sap that transmits life. It boils, it does violence to the leaf that is modeled beneath its effort. Who made this masterpiece? An anonymous Gothic artist formed those beautiful openings, those cast or projected shadows! Does anyone understand how much grandeur there is in the lumps and holes by which the simple portrait of a plant is made? There is indeed so much grandeur that these holes and lumps are on a par with the highest thoughts. In other words, Nature is there in her fullness, sensitive nature, outcome of all the forces that work in secret.

Yes, a single law; everywhere the same harmony. A common spirit unites all these works. What modesty they advise to us! What light they bring to our thoughts!

I look and cannot go away. I am surrounded by these lights; some of them fade into the distance; others vibrate very close to me.

These fragments are ancient. But, whether French or Greek, the same feeling, the same sphinx of beauty, prevails. In one or the other Nature is always transposed and resuscitated. And this same transposition makes the supreme splendor of Egypt and of India. I see all this as through tears of joy. And when I am weary of admiring man. I turn toward the landscape and savor profoundly convalescence from that affliction: the City.

To return to truth, to turn again to nature, and to principles: this is to relink the present with the past. Instinct recognizes instinct beyond intervening gaps.

To bind the present with the past is the necessary action. In so doing one will restore wisdom and happiness to the living. Those who possess happiness because they have bowed down to truth, do not wish to reserve that treasure for themselves alone. Unconsciously, all humanity hungers and thirsts for it. There is a misunderstanding between the past and the present.

The artist ought to be listened to.

Not imitated! He himself does not imitate, he does not wish to be imitated. Even in order to approach the Antique, he does not resort to copying. He adopts the means the Ancients used: the study of nature.

Not imitated: but heeded!

He, the docile confident of nature, lives among quite other marvels than those of the Thousand and One Nights. He can teach the masses the art of admiring, thus providing them with magnificent and countless opportunities for development and happiness.

We rejoice in an infinite richness of life on condition that we submit joyously to the true Laws—those that man does not decree but which are the eternal texts, eternally offered to his eyes, his mind, and his heart. What a paradise this earth is! Let us not speak of evil, which we do not understand. Let us try only to exhaust the share of good, of happiness, that we inherit: we shall not be able to exhaust it, for it is infinite. And it is clearly given to us.

Beauty, like the air, costs nothing. The earth, calm or troubled, in bloom or showing its skeleton, the seasons, the animals and flowers, the city crowds, the admirable portraits you see in an autobus, a boat, or a train; everywhere, artist, you find food to nourish your hunger for beauty. What matter if, from afar, you cannot distinguish a face? The general movement indicates it to you; and if you see only the face, that indicates the general movement. A countenance and a bearing reveal the whole story of a person, a whole novel written in the flesh. And since this law of beauty is not conventional, you will venerate it in the face of your enemy himself— if you can endure the sight of him—and this holds even for beings whose race is hostile to your own. Animals are worthy of our homage, and it is right that the horse becomes the equal of the rider in an equestrian monument. There is not so much as a blade of grass that is not "articulated in beauty." One must only observe, while intervening the least possible, in order not to disturb the actors of this drama and not to *denature* them. Formerly I chose my models and indicated their poses. I have long ago left that error behind. All models are infinitely beautiful, and their spontaneous gestures are those that one feels are the most divine. Whenever beauty reveals itself to me, multiplying from moment to moment according to my degree of better understanding, I begin to work— as soon as my pencil is sharpened or my clay pliable—studying what I see, what is given me, indeed certain that it would be superfluous to choose.

In this state of mind, when one feels that he participates in nature, how could he fail to be happy?

It is in this joy that the artist today wishes to commune with all men as he did long ago in the Cathedral, for there is a place and a part for all. This joy is immense and yet belongs wholly to whoever wishes to make the effort to lay hold on it. One of the natural laws is that all should be for all: does not each one of us brim the sky? I do not exaggerate. A woman who combs her hair fills the sky with her gesture. And it is impossible for us to make any movement that is devoid of beauty. It is equally impossible to section or limit our thoughts and their shades of meaning, which may be translated by gestures that are boundless in number and fullness. We have then, all of us, immensity for our province.

This conviction augments our stature by permitting us to take pride in the place nature has in her heart for us! Her generosity should awaken our gratitude. Art is the expression of that gratitude, praise of nature by man fills all with love and admiration before her.

Art is the harmonious rite of that great religion of nature.

If the artist were heeded, all men would be reconciled in that religion, and beauty created by man would be understood, would be sacred, by the same token as the beauty of the sky or of the sea.

The heavens declare the glory of God:* the Cathedrals join to that the glory of man. They offer all men a splendid, comforting, and exalting spectacle; the spectacle of ourselves, the eternalized image of our soul, of our country, of all that by opening our eyes, we have learned to love.

When the artist is listened to, we shall cease to be blind to the familial magnificences of these monuments that bear the monogram of France, no longer deaf to the accent of these chimes that speak our language.

Hope rings from the high belfries of our Cathedrals.

The benevolence of nature and the courage of the artist will succeed in reestablishing all in order.

* Psalm 19:1

So much ardor lies hidden in these old monuments. They are essentially so young. In studying them, I recover my youth.

For my contemporaries I am a *bridge* connecting two banks, the past to the present. Often I have seen crowds hesitate before enormous Gothic piles, asking themselves if they are truly beautiful. May they deign to accept me as guarantee, with Ruskin and so many other masters, when we affirm that this architecture is of sublime beauty. Oh, that I might put an end to the misunderstanding that turns away the very ones to whom this beauty is dedicated!

Why do we—universally, I believe—admire the Greeks, Egyptians, Persians? Does the rarity of their works confer an added value? Have they not gained more merit and dignity from each one of the wounds that time has made? Then mark this: the violences committed by vandals of all times, and the dark acts practiced in our time, have given the martyred monuments of the Middle Ages the distinctive seal of rarity which you relish in those of Persia, Egypt, and Greece.

I have already said that strokes of violence are not mortal. They must be condemned, that is understood, they must be prevented, and I wish that someone would bring French municipal administrators to see our old churches, that they might be made to understand the *value* of these hands, these faces, these folds of drapery, of these wholes which they destroy.

But against an absolutely beautiful work, the vandal cannot prevail unless he reduces it to dust; the plane endures, and, thanks to that, I reconstitute the whole, removing the wound from my sight.

Nor can the blows of time deprive us of Beauty. Time is infinitely just and wise. Its action over our works wears them, but it returns almost as much as it takes away. If time attenuates the details, it adds to the planes a new grandeur, a venerable character.

The true enemies of architecture and sculpture are the bad architects and sculptors, the great, fashionable surgeons who claim to "remake," artificially, the limbs that the patient has lost. Oh, those artists who make art "by deliberation"! and by imitation!

One must study, study himself.

What I myself do is a small matter and occupies little space. But the accomplishments of our ancestors. It extends over our land! You can see it everywhere about us. And I have this merit: I have seen it in order to be able to speak of it to you, that I might inspire you in turn with a desire to see it. The people have not the means to undertake such studies; they serve in other ways. Our "workers" haven't the leisure to burrow into this new Herculaneum, the Cathedral. I have done that for them. By my years of labor I feel I have become the brother of other workers, the brother of those great laborers. I should be happy if they were willing to accept the fruit of my work, my experience.

Thus I take by the hand the pride of each one of our provinces and cities, and in Paris from whence they may radiate beyond the limits of the nation, I gather these riches together. They belong to all! Each one may say to himself, "I am rich."

It is not that I claim to have understood everything. Oh, no! I have admitted my mistakes; I could cite many others. There are so many beauties in this beauty! However strong the impression experienced may be, it is never definitive. At first glance one is astonished, the mind makes efforts, enormous bounds, to assimilate the thought of the artist. But the law remains beyond and, like clouds which rise over the horizon, observations continue to accumulate. I observe, striving to decompose, to recompose, as one who tests. For twenty years I have been doing that, living each time by a small discovery, a flash of comprehension, and I no longer count upon the conquest of the absolute.

Knowledge does not give all of herself to one man. I yield to this thought; I am a small link in a chain. May I have contributed to bringing back light and discipline in art! And may I be heard when I *preach* simplicity as the prime condition of happiness and of beauty. It is true that simplicity is difficult to attain; all that we are, all that we do, is in relationship with nature as a whole. Thus it is of nature as a whole that one must always think. Is that possible? But nature as a whole is nevertheless there, before me, in the model, a true point or a multitude of true points. Let us observe the model attentively, it will tell us all.

In the cities we have unfortunately reached such a state of feverish excitement that nature has great trouble calming us. As for me, I am still impatient with men's passions. Perhaps it is well to always be crossed by affliction, that we may not become sluggish.

My new friend, old age—which my contemporaries have made so beautiful for me!—gives me certainties that I should like, in return, to share with all.

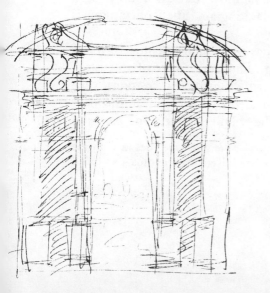

CHAPTER THREE

Remarks on the Romanesque Style

GOTHIC ART is the history of France.* It is the tree of all our genealogies. It presides over our formation as it lives in our transformations. It persists in the styles that follow it as far as the end of the 18th century. These styles are its declensions.

Because the Romanesque style comes from the catacombs of the first Christians, who lived in thick, hidden crypts, it is a humble and somber style, like the birth of its religion.

Romanesque architecture is always more or less a cave or a heavy crypt. Art is a prisoner there, lacking air. The Romanesque is the chrysalis of the Gothic.

As order required, this chrysalis has only such essential forms as one sees illustrated in a perfect being. Those forms are of an austere simplicity with a binding, a border which girds and festoons, running around one window, to begin again further on at the next window, and so on, engarlanding the whole edifice. One can find

*Translator's note: For Rodin Gothic art or "le gothique" began with the first French kings and lasted through the French Renaissance; thus it included the Romanesque.

this beautiful decorative simplicity in the trimming of a cope.*

The Gothic, even at the time of its greatest prodigality of ornament, has never failed to recognize the Romanesque principle. That principle is French. The Gothic evolves from the Romanesque as a flower evolves from a bud.

The Romanesque Porch.

Its arches are superimposed, and the arrangement of these superimpositions is carved with very simple motifs, almost childish designs. There is no subject. These are ornamented moldings and, for almost everyone, they are without interest, negligible, crude.

"What a mistake! We would never do that again!" they say. Yet, it is as though one heard Aeschylus or Homer himself.

We claim, I know, to put more intellect into our complications than there is in this "barbarous" work. But this barbarous work has a sublime accent.

We are mistaken.

The ancients were concerned with determining the masses of shadows, then with piercing and ornamenting them according to a goal. We chisel ornaments that are foreign to every general line and which do not enter the great stream of harmony. To the eyes

* *Translator's note:* ecclesiastical mantle.

of those who truly see, the plane is the principal matter; that is why, in their work, it is always very beautiful. It engenders Merovingian shadows, violent and strong, rough and wild.

Such is the grandiose Romanesque art. It is the geometry of beauty. Epochs which we persist in treating as barbarous possessed that scientific tradition. We have lost it.

The Romanesque is the father of French styles. Full of reserve and energy, it produced all our architecture. The future must still and always be mindful of the Romanesque principle. This style, the egg containing the germ of life, was perfect from its primitive phase, and the horn of abundance is not emptied; it is inexhaustible.

The Romanesque comes from the Roman. It has conserved that discipline which the Romans doubtless received from the Greeks and the Greeks from the Egyptians. This discipline, the vertebral column of all art capable of enduring, is a geometry drawn from primitive sources in nature and in her laws. It has been preserved up to our time in order that one day we might have remembrance.

But when indeed shall we cease insulting the past, we who have miserably lost its magnificent virtues? We no longer know what a plane is, either in sculpture or in architecture, that drawing of the depths, that drawing of shadow, that proportioning of shadow. From this our contrary judgments derive.

These staircases, so long and so numerous, these pilasters of buttresses in graduated steps, to be admired, for example, at Chartres; the horizontal and the perpendicular evolving according to regulated values: these constitute the Gothic, which was founded upon the buttress. And that buttress is nothing else than the simple and rampant Romanesque buttress, perforated and chiseled.

After a period of four centuries, as a plant that had long been compressed gravely rises upon its stem, the Romanesque, a rather low plant, drew itself up in small columns and became the Gothic. Clarity was added to the admirable, primitive conciseness.

A column which, in mounting to its full height, has capitals twice over; power that reasserts itself after renewal; two nodes like those on certain stems, such as those of rush or of wheat.

Sturdy arches, carried by sturdy columns; arches where the nave opens with elegant columns: Noah's Ark.

MELUN · ON ENTERING this old church, it seems to me that I enter my soul. My most personal daydreams arise and come to me when I push open the door.

Yet the impression is that of a crypt, of a tomb.

What silence! How far one is from everything!

But traces of light at the other end permit and counsel hope. The heavy silence that seems to uphold these thick columns is the atmosphere needed for thought.

This silence, moreover, vibrates like light. It is the expression, the soul, of this austere and profound art.

Two columns near the chancel, coupled, one might say, on one base, appear to me like two angels. They have a triumphal character. They are two great witnesses of the power and purity that have their sanctuary here. And to the heaviness of the edifice they bring an ineffable lightness. Suddenly it happens that in contemplating them ever more lovingly, I grow, I participate in their nature. Emanations of purity and of strength come to me from them. The youth of my soul revives. I receive baptism a seond time and I emerge happier, more enamoured of divine glory and of human genius.

Save for the capitals, no ornament is in this church. Here are only masses, cubes, right angles. The unique element of variety is brought by high, narrow columns rising to the apex in low relief on these cubes, on these massive pillars, powerful supports of this church atop which, so solid it is, one might build another church.

And is this not the historical reality? Has not the Gothic church been built upon the Romanesque church?

Therein lies a terrible knowledge. In this austere style, nothing is invented or willed by men who could have willed differently. All is interlocked. Creators are spirits more obedient than others, and the centuries are governed by long thoughts.

I feel happy and subdued like a woman before her master. By truth surprised, I am in a transport of joy. How far I live from my time! I must make an effort to remember that a short while ago I was in the street, a contemporary street, an actual one. My true sustenance is here, in this cave. It is here that my entire life and my constant studies come to focus. All my anterior efforts converged to open this seventh heaven to me! I know not what I might experience at Athens or in Egypt. Could it be more?

I must add that in the past I had already entered this same church and found it sad and cold. But since then I have acquired more understanding and more tenderness, with more years.

The portal, remade in the 16th century, is infinitely graceful; in architectural ornamentation, it is the equivalent of the poetry of the Pléiade.

On the tympanum, only ornaments remain, exquisite in themselves. But formerly there were, no doubt, figures of a higher interest. A warbling of birds has succeeded a profound symphony of the forest.

Later that will be reduced to a cartouche; where a whole story was developed, we shall see no more than a coat of arms, and yet certain traces of this divine story will persist.

Still later these traces, these momentoes of the grand style, will go in the greater part of our cities, to beautify the dwellings of certain private persons with the somber elegance and peaceful nobility of these façades, these doors.

This flowering expression of the French spirit, this intellectual well-being that distinguished our race, is the final form of Gothic art retouched by the genius of the Renaissance.

But here are children coming into the church. Then, a few minutes later, they leave, playing. They are like the exquisite Renaissance ornaments that have been added to the portal. Who knows if perhaps these children may have retained something from this catechism of stone? Happier, more wise than their parents who pass in front of the church without entering, without seeing it.

Shall not a generation come that is capable of hearing me, I who cease not to repeat: the truth of art and happiness are here!

I write for that generation.

CHAPTER FOUR

Etampes

LODGED FOR A FEW DAYS not far from the church, I go to sleep and awake with my thoughts of it. At the ringing of the Angelus my life of travel begins. Soon, and until evening, I shall be under a spell of enchantment before this unique jewel in a city where all else has been dishonored by municipal barbarism.

A man who lived ten centuries ago comes to life again in me. Is there a nobility of mind that is transmitted through the centuries, as there is a nobility of blood? Or am I too presumptuous? No. I owe all my development to art.

This winsome church is not large. But what a belfry! What grace it had yesterday in the moonlight!

This is a belfry *en fer de lance*. The expansions are effected by small perforated towers and slender cloumns. A great wall forms a large, wide repose: this is the façade of one side. This wall is enriched by a black portal *in both high and low relief*. This portal, very different from Gothic portals because of its projections, somewhat recalls an ancient sarcophagus.

For I had forgotten to tell you that this little church is Romanesque. Its saints and its teachers, very elongated, rise beside the portal and on the tympanum of the portal. It is impossible not to recognize in them the true pillars of the Church. The sharpness of the ordered folds of their tunics and their measured gestures bespeak their certitude and the power of their spirit as much as the small ornaments crushed beneath their feet proclaim their victory over passions and vices. The arcade of the tympanum rises above them, and the saints appear spaced like planets in the half circumference of the three heavens.

They still belong to us! May they never join the "collections"! May they never be torn from this portal and sold to allow for the passage of blind Progress!

But all is to be feared since these marvels that have been the glory of so many centuries are as if nonexistent for our contemporaries. And how, even here, avoid the thought of violence where it has left much of its harmful imprint? A few juttings are scratched, a few capitals are shattered. The supports of the statues of saints and their draperies are mutilated.

The iconoclasts have returned with the princes of the church, with the architects, the restorers, and the city advisors.

I enter the church once more; I have sought and found again the joy always granted me by this sweet combat between the shades of night and mystical clarity. I wish to relive that moment.

My thought, caressed by the chants, waves and unwinds like a charmed snake and is astonished, at first, by the darkness. The threshold crossed, a single impression is dominant: a sense of the grandiose in this night, knowingly organized and deepened.

But now, from the back, windows pierce the wall with lights. I begin to see.

Down there candles seem to make a flaming crown of intellectual flowers that burn without movement.

The columns have just appeared in their calm arrangement; they grow even more tranquil as they approach me. They withdraw when I have passed, becoming iridescent as they cross at the back and return on the other side, alike, yet never identical inasmuch as I see them from various distances. I imagine I contemplate white virgins of a procession passing close to me along their way, effacing themselves, then reappearing after having accomplished the rite. All in this miraculous art has a life at once sacred and human. And by what simple means the effects are composed and executed!

My eyes adapt to darkness. The real order of things is revealed. But the poetry has lost nothing by this reality.

At the back of the apse, the stained-glass windows are calm stars in the firmament. Such windows remind one also of flowers, of true flowers where there are true stained-glass windows.

How sweet the shadow is! It seems to rock the chants from the depth of the chancel. And distance transforms the stained glass into frescoes that are slightly rubbed out.

What harmony! How one would like to carry it with one as a defense against the world's hostile incoherence!

Motionless lights illumine the distance and I make out the throng of the faithful.

A woman comes, thrilling with youth beneath her long, black veils; her lines undulate, varied by the draperies. Another, absent-minded and charming, moves her lips; I am not sure she is praying. At times currents from the congregation cross each other, broken by the rapid steps of women who are like arrows loosed by grace.

For a long time one heard voices coming in the distance, alternating, interlacing their rhythms; they come nearer. This is the procession approaching, and here it is.

First three young men, graceful as the muses. One bears the cross, two others carry candlesticks; their gestures have the gentleness and firmness of those who are seen carved on tympanums. Their costume also is ancient, happily, and the slow moving verses are answered in its folds.

Next come young girls led by a religious, a magnificent example of humanity: severe, straight, beautiful as the caryatid of duty.

Nothing to say of the men, the priests, with features lacking distinction, and with their closed physiognomy from which sympathy turns away. I note simply in their group two grown choir boys swinging the thurible: fortunate gestures, so measured, so controlled!

This is the great moment. The congregation chants its heart in the prayer—verses, antiphons, and recitatives. It appears to be mute, but it has delegated its voice. On behalf of all, the mature man and the child address heaven with admirable chants that are like the actual high reliefs of the sanctuary where saints, aligned on the arches, welcome them.

How they love sculpture, these Cathedrals! They inspire in women a taste for beautiful drapery, advising them to ask of stiff folds an increase of beauty, for modesty and chastity are the elder sisters of beauty, and the Cathedrals know this.

Is there not everywhere here a magnificent eulogy to woman formulated in the plastic language of stone?* And if the Virgin is first to be honored by it, is it not she who opens to us the gates of springtime? Do we not discover the universe thanks to her?

* *Translator's note:* Stone (*pierre*) is correct in this context, although the French word is "*prière*" (prayer), a typographical error.

Have you never stopped, your spirit and heart in suspense, abashed to have discovered this masterpiece: a woman at prayer? A woman never loses the line, mother of the grace which God has conferred on her, which always lends her a supernatural character and inspires in us the desire to place a crown on her head. Ah, those who have penetrated the most mysterious and most intimate depths of delight are well aware that they have a beyond and, in that beyond, woman possesses us still! After having glimpsed this woman at prayer in the church, did you not withdraw and then discretely come back without allowing yourself to be seen, to revel in this good fortune, to admire this attitude in such perfect harmony with the nave as a whole, this ample frame destined for this unique portrait? And can you say that this woman and her natural genius are inferior to any of the most incontestable marvels of art? Is she not in herself a perfect architecture? Do not the columns of the temple form for her a cortege as would the beautiful trees in a garden of love?

In the Cathedrals all women are Polymnias. All their movements belong to beauty. This architecture projects its glory over them as a tribute of gratitude. See on the tympanum the coronation of the Virgin: how well the artist who conferred so much chaste emotion upon this beautiful figure knew that a drapery of shadow is necessary to an expression of the divinity of souls!

In leaving I wanted to study again my great bas-relief of the portal that resembles a sarcophagus on a high battlemented wall.

There I judge the height to be seven meters with an equal width; one meter of projection for the buttress on the wall; slightly more depth at the portal, the double perhaps.

The shadow is sharply modeled in black around the figures that are hewn as if by a punch; this is what gives the portal an aspect of low-relief, high-relief. Without excess of grace, the portal has not the dryness of the Arab-Byzantine style because the curves of the archivolt overhang the projections in bias and regulate the shadow.

Nevertheless there is in this style a severity from which the sweetness of the Gothic rests us. Justice, austerity, and discipline are affirmed in these arrested protrusions, limited in their flight; an arrested impetus which will surge up later. The energy of belief will become the sensual delight of believing; discipline will flower in joy.

The great concern of Gothic artists, in which they differed from those of the Romanesque period, was to ask suppleness of detail from the calculated conflict between light and shadow. This bas-relief is rather more Romanesque; here the black is chiseled. But how majestic it is in its naïve barbarism and power!

Whether Gothic or Romanesque, our Cathedrals are always sublime by that wisdom of proportions which is at once the essential virtue above all others and the splendor of nature and of art.

You see in this church at Etampes how the large walls, by the silence of their surfaces, prepare the eloquent effect of the portal, and the singing effect of the belfry, so compact and yet so open.

The adorable genius of man, which for centuries confided to the caresses of the stars all his love, all his faith, all his labor in a single motif of glory!

The Cathedrals are my magical muses; they instruct, while they charm me.

CHAPTER FIVE

Mantes

THE LITTLE HOTEL ROOM where I slept is all surrounded by love. Its atmosphere prepares me for communion with nature. I have emerged from my night, and a morning walk has once more restored my hope and my love.

Let us go to the masterpiece!

The city is nonexistent. This small, entirely materialistic city turns to the capital for its ideas. How wrong it is! The capital has long since lost its old power, and the changing convulsions satisfy no more than selfish interests.

There is nothing here but the ruins of Notre Dame, splendid and immense.

This afternoon the sun is playing in this church. It escapes; it returns. Here the light inscribes many things.

Very often it attenuates Gothic hardness by its alliance with shadow; thus it accompanies the artist's thought.

Like a fan, the sun changes places. Like an artist, it paints with rapid strokes, running toward what calls to it.

However, this powerful god could do nothing for a bad modern work, and nothing with the thought of a mediocre architect. From such work and such thought, light could extricate no more than boredom.

But to receive the sun, one must have dwelt for a long while in its thrice-blessed courts. One must have gone to meet it for a long while, must long have been its student. As to bad monuments, the sun has nothing to say to bad artists whom the open air of the work-yards has not prepared with understanding.

Is it possible that everyone is oblivious to, or mistakes, the sun's gifts? Does it not present the universe with majesty, making every-thing perceptible and living? Does it not inspire the poet, whether famous or obscure? The sun is responsible for the prosperity of farmers, the joy of animals, the fertility of the land; and man's thoughts perhaps have their principle and their hearth in its light and warmth. For a long time man believed he saw God's truth blazing in its fires, and God wishes us to adore the sun. When it shines, the earth is modeled according to its divine flame.

Thus it is allowed and, by patience and diligence, it is possible to understand and feel the geometry of light. In this the spirit tastes repose in silence, drawing from it a new energy and generosity.

Light that is governed inside churches by stained-glass windows, depends upon them and judges them. Here, for example, is a bad window, a modern work which usurps the place of an ancient marvel. Light coming through it jostles the peace of the place and disturbs the proportions. This stained glass suggests storm, while the Cathedral itself is a day of fine weather.

Conversely, a whole other part of the church is truly bathed in the sky because in that part there are no restored windows. The old windows keep in harmony with the sky. The new ones are for bathrooms and exhibition palaces. They are cold despite their violent spots.

Mentally I spread this one on the ground: it is an oriental rug whose openings are of the sky.

That one is a pack of playing cards. Kings, Queens, Jacks. What a shame that great subjects should henceforth be treated and made by the methods of an inferior industry! Thus the church has come to reproduce commercially the idols that primitive peoples adored.

Certain windows seem inspired by Japanese art: they are exquisite; others by Chinese art: they are austere.

I must return to the subject of *breaks* and *restorations*.

The artist need not worry about broken places; generally, far from diminishing works, they are an *addition*.

At least they never *disturb*.

It is the repairs that produce disorder. A broken area is always the work of chance; well, chance is always favorable to art. If one attempted to break *neatly* and to *clean up*, that would be abominable. Therefore it is not of the iconoclasts that I complain, but of the restorers.

See the Renaissance fountain at Mantes. For three centuries children had battered it; it was still beautiful. Now it is repaired in the bourgeois manner and therefore no more than an exhibition stucco, suitable for a garden in the style of simulated stone, without modeling, no longer effective.

The restoration of churches strips them of their style. Their capitals become flabby and heavy. They take on a character of town halls, of municipal buildings. Their form, in its entirety and in its detail, is outraged, afflicted.

Products of a sick France, of a France ravaged by selfish interest, of that France of the schools where people talk and no longer know how to work.

The exquisite raiment of other times falls; the mask is torn like a beautiful veil. One no longer knows.

The evil comes from schools, from museums. It is useless to seek

TONNERRE · 121

124 · CHAMPEAUX

126 · SENS

knowledge in museums; they are only for our pleasure. If you really wish to learn, work alone with nature. Observe her directly, with your own eyes. After that, you may go to museums; you will be at home there. Those who begin with museums will remain eternal copyists, translators who destroy the spirit, being without initiative, they cannot understand.

Do you know what the *original* is in the mind of our contemporaries? It is the *odd*, the unmated. The Ancients never allowed that barbarous conception to be born. The holy populations of their nations did not allow their character to be attenuated. They saw in art an equilibrium of forces borrowed from nature, that is to say, from a higher reason than our own.

To obey that reason, rather than to correct it by an artificial calculation, is to assimilate oneself with those infallible forces which the artist wields without understanding. It is to enter nature's secret. Let us be as simple as the Ancients. The more simple we are, the more we shall be complete, for simplicity signifies unity in truth.

Study in the schools is study of the frontal view, that is to say, of illusion. The very aspect of man, as well as his mind, reproves that error. The frontal view is the result of divers profiles. The plane of each one of these profiles is simple. To achieve that simplicity, requires a long and patient practice.

Moreover, life is before us in an aspect that we have calumnied.

We no longer know how to understand this living tableau of serene grandeurs. We pass without seeing it. Our misfortune is that in our giddiness we wish to retouch Nature. Our contrariety betrays our powerlessness.

And yet, what joy and what succor nature lavishes on the one who knows how to see and to admire! To admire is to live in God. It is to know heaven, that heaven which is always ill described because always looked for too far away: it is here, like happiness, very near to us! Anything will suggest its real presence to you, provided you are intelligent and sensitive. Begin by studying a plant, the first that comes along, and soon you will disdain all the childishness of selfish interests and all the superficiality of ambitions.

Very often we say that the weather is bad: what do we know about that?

Once again it is the whole that we should be able to judge. Have patience while waiting to understand and, in the first place, admire. Everything is admirable, even that which wounds us. To revolt against nature is a vain waste of strength; it stems from ignorance and ends in suffering.

Ah! *bad* weather, isn't it? It's a dark day with the sky like a threatening sea that overhangs and is going to fall. How beautiful it is!

Let us have as our basic certainty the idea that nature is beautiful in its entirety, and, armed by this principle, let us observe; we shall have grown when we recognize the grandeur of aspects that formerly shocked us. But, like all conquests, this one costs an effort of which we are no longer capable.

Why so much flaccidness, so much feebleness in what we still call taste, our taste? It is because we live in a time that is more concerned with materiality than with spirit, in which taste in art is abolished. We scorn to devote real powers to art. How can you expect that our self-styled artists, never having taken the trouble to study in the light of day, could, when they dabble at restoring Gothic monuments, respectfully treat these magnificent examples of life? They block what should be open to the light. They are incapable of comparing, of understanding, being too hurried.

To study, one must go slowly, deserting the agitated century, and resign oneself in advance to not making a fortune.

We no longer have time to study. There are no more apprentices. The craftsman, although he knew the benefit he had from his own apprenticeship, has not formed new apprentices. The centuries-old chain is broken. Work! Are there still men who work? Yes; there are some. But what good is it, since work is said to lead to nothing?

You are mistaken! Work leads to happiness first of all. Still more: it leads to contemplation of God, perhaps, seen through His veils. And for the worker, work kills jealousy. The man who knows the recompense of work rises above base passions. He applauds the success of his colleagues. He is grateful to the genius who survives in works and in countless progeny. Work is a perpetual rejuvenation. It relates us with the animals who are our true brothers, with the trees, with all plants, the most humble as well as the most sumptuous. What beautiful friends we have in vegetable plants! In what way are lettuce or celery plants less beautiful than "ornamental" plants—so named by a word that misleads by being exclusive? The potato blossom is a princely flower; observe it on the costumes of the time of Louis XVI: what more gracious ornament?

Then let us reinstate all things in our admiration and not look so far afield for beauty. There is enough within the frame of our window to nourish enthusiasm. Look out of your own window. Observe your family and your friends. Admire the touching beauty of those dear faces wherein the soul's silent sacrifice appears as through a transparent veil. See your friends as Rembrandt saw his. Do you suppose there were none but living masterpieces about that great man? The point is that he possessed the virtue of work. What a miraculous tool of comprehension! It is only a matter of your learning how to handle it.

Man is unhappy because he attempts to escape from the law of work, because he wishes to play, like boys and ambitious men, at who is to be the leader, the first. Thus he betrays his own intelligence, which does not demand the joys of vanity. His natural object is truth; his natural activity is the effort by which he may attain to that truth in the hidden world and understand its workings. The radiant result of that effort is happiness. Happiness, like a running horse, accompanies the questing intellect. But it is ever to the depths that one must quest. When I say that the human body has so much varied beauty, so much grandeur, I presume as evident truth that the soul enclosed in this masterpiece is itself the crowning of the whole and its mistress. Let us discover the soul in the body.

I know neither India nor China. But I love the French countryside. I can speak of it, even though one should suspect the prejudice of my affection.

How delicate are our French horizons! They have a sweetly monotonous grandeur like the goodness that inspires intelligence and makes a joy of every act of life. Life is measured in the country. It has its own rhythm. The race is there; genius is there; there is goodness in innocence; and there is gradual wisdom. Even bad things are made good by a country environment. Ideas return, so to speak, to the earth and come back to us in better health. The peasant does not hurry; he keeps step with the centuries.

We must know how to retrace our steps. Impatient people never agree to that. Anything rather than to begin again! Poor folk! They are sworn to irremediable ignorance, for patience is the first condition of all fruitful study.

How well adversity teaches us that indispensable patience! Thereby adversity is our benefactor. It is the only serious school we have left, and it is wide open to us at this time. We are caught in the trap of our vanity, of our ridiculous ambition. But in that good school adversity, we learn the real value of things and all that books do not know. So is the counterweight released by our own faults and without our knowledge.

This precious teaching of patience might be heard everywhere if we knew how to listen.

Through example, all women teach us patience, effortlessly adding heroism thereto. Alas, is it only in the past that one may appropriately praise women in this way? Swept on to her own downfall by that of man, woman today is disoriented; with a frightening rapidity she loses her ancestral virtues; she is wrong.

How moving and charming the drama of a household in which woman played the role of guardian angel! Let us not despair. She still knows how to love. What power for expansion she has within her when she loves. How she invents life. And how unconquerable when she defends her nest!

This church, this immense creature is a "centipede."

The tympanum of the center portal.
The Christ and the Virgin have been ravaged. In its battered state this bas-relief seems retouched by Michelangelo. It has gained in beauty; chance, that serves poor people so well, has also served this sculpture. Some blacks have been cut off, and their effects from a distance appear more collected.

On this bas-relief of the tympanum, one finds again the character of an antique sarcophagus. There is an equal simplification of effects, so appropriate to the immensity of the building.

The elect are on the right, the condemned on the left. The elect form a single block without opening or division; the bas-relief is compact. The reproved also form a block, but the movement of their legs allows something like perforations below the tunics: this is the only impression of openwork in the whole composition besides the important effect of the base which separates it from the lower bas-relief. Below, black festoons cast a shadow.

I can barely distinguish the second bas-relief: a few impressions, again black festoons with shadows beneath. And yet, I feel this is also beautiful.

But the third bas-relief is greater. The saints in the starry arches evoke the immense vault of the real stars. What I see of that larger relief has an Attic grandeur. The Antique continues to exist here. Its immortal wisdom is found, that wisdom which no longer satisfies our poor, ailing minds. Once again this truth is proven to me: there is no enduring originality other than taste and order.

This third door is almost Byzantine. What science! This is an Asiatic memento: the mummy of a great humanity; its draperies are really shrouds. Women are here, as in a chorus of Aeschylus, passionless, immovable, the head barely inclined. A single one lifts her forearm; all other lines are close. The angels are Assyrian, without softness, without kindness. The large sleeve of one of them suggests the gesture of a powerful beast. There are also Assyrian movements in the adoring angel and in the one who swings the thurible. The draped Christ radiates from his throne. The movement of his open, parted arms distributes justice. His drapery, according to tradition, recalls a toga. A rising dance rhythm lifts the angels, despite the tight folds of their tunics and although their legs remain together.

One senses in these attitudes laws that cannot be transgressed, that are implacable and abstract like the *Credo* which is the monument, the cornerstone, and basis of religion. These laws are a State justification; they declare all modification heretical.

The ornaments are almost all in Byzantine style. The figures themselves are subject to that style: the human being is elongated to the length of a column. In this one may see an appearance of barbarism, but no more than an appearance, for the synthesis is always right. The essential is there. A superior geometry presides over the ordering of these figures and these ornaments.

In the foliated scrolls, man tests his strength in combat with birds and with lions. For them, and above them, there is only light and shade. Only the divine is above human, animal, and vegetable life. At first, people were satisfied by festoons standing out against the wall, by ornamentation bordering the doors and windows. Subject matter did not come until later. In time, the subject rose to God. Then man replaced God, and since then all has to be recommenced.

I have just seen a Renaissance church in which the square buttress, the round tower, and the wall gave the impression of a molding "doucine." This proves that the largest form may effect one in the same way as the smallest.

Broad lights and wide horizons. The train that follows the railroad tracks seems to juggle with artificial clouds in fleeing away.

My gaze returns to the main road. How I love all things, all manifestations of life that I meet here! A small house along the border, a charming collection of simple folk. But here comes an automobile. From a distance it has seen a man cross the road. It comes down upon him like anger! It is irritated by all that passes in front of it.

I continue my way. One may begin from one end or the other; it's all the same, always beauty in agreement with Nature. There is no beginning: light comes as soon as one sets off.

CHAPTER SIX

Nevers

THIS CATHEDRAL is the scaffolding of heaven.

It gathers itself for flight; it rises, then stops the first time to rest on the balustrade of the first tier; then the construction resumes its skyward flight. It stops at the limit of human powers.

I collect my thoughts usefully and joyously only in the open air of façades, in the shadow of naves, and in the wealth of bright mornings.

I am lord of my life today.

In these beautiful masses of shadow, these beautiful masses of light, these beautiful bodies of half light, what energy! Gothic genius models all that. And in my veins I feel the Gothic sap moving like the earth's juices flowing through the plants. This is the blood of our fathers, who were such great artists! How rare today are the minds initiated into their geometry which is all human wisdom, all consciousness! But new generations will come after the torment that we traverse; they will pay these stones, sacred because they are all impregnated with a thought that cannot die, the tribute of veneration which is their due.

From first glance, what a profound impression this majestic order imposes upon me! It is little short of perfection.

This depth, which is the moral beauty of architecture, is offered here in all its richness.

The beams of light that cross the interior of the building enliven its solitude.

What a mistake to believe that the Gothic style is constituted by the ogival, or lancet, arch! The church of Saint-Etienne of Nevers has an absolutely semicircular arch: thus Romanesque? No! All the essential characteristics of the Gothic style are there, and no single detail is sufficient to characterize a whole.

This Romanesque decoration composed of great, deep, superimposed niches is reminiscent of a columbarium.

A bridge of blind arcades, that is, an exterior buttress, comes to consolidate the walls. Above, short columns, strong and thick with

heavy heads; their blind arcades, willfully animated, seem to be caryatids.

This nave is inundated by a filtered light, the one that Raphael
loved. And there are also lights in the manner of Clouet.

The Greeks above all, and ahead of us, understood this magic of
light. The Gothics rediscovered it for themselves because it is in
the nature of man to adore the effects of the sun and to express them
by leading them in their natural direction. Here the effect is attained
by the firmness which the small columns accentuate.

The spirit that created the Parthenon is the same spirit that created
the Cathedrals. Divine beauty! Only here there is more refinement.
There is, dare I say, a luminous mist wherein the unscored light sleeps
as in the vales. Those who have visited these naves during the morning hours understand me.

These three niches, triple motive for enthusiasm!

Everywhere, however, I breathe an atmosphere of humidity, of
humility, smelling of a prison. It recalls my mind to this initial
thought: suffering, sacrifice, love—which produced the Cathedral.

The exterior apse of this church with these small agglomerated chapels and the higher one which groups them, recalls Hadrian's Tomb.

The adorable, astonished Virgin: the babe seeks the breast, but she absently plays with him forgetting, because she is not yet fully a mother, that she must nurse him.

At the back of the chancel, the dark of the Holy of Holies gives a more vital intensity to the golden blaze of the suspended lamps. Nowhere else than in the Cathedrals has this magic light of the crypts been so lovingly treated. This light shines on the tiles. It projects reflections, bars of clarity that cross the massive shadows horizontally and in bias. Everywhere here this magic of light, this queen of chiaroscuro, is at home.

Behind the altar, the shadow thickens in the apse divided into honeycomb cells. This is the grange where the wheat sleeps. It is the cave from which some day the Lord's wine shall flow. The only source of light in these dark chapels, these tombs, are the small stained-glass windows, where the martyrdom of Saint Stephen is traced in a violent drawing that stands out against an angelic blue.

Louis XIV had added to this church wrought-iron grilles of magnificent elegance that harmonized with the building as a whole, for the style of Louis XIV is a declension of the Gothic. It was beautiful. In place of those Louis XIV grilles, a new Gothic grille, a caricature of the Gothic, has been substituted. It is ugly. This is the letter, but not the spirit, of the Gothic; therefore, in reality it is not at all Gothic, since what is ugly belongs to no style.

Tonnerre.

For our delight this masterpiece has been neglected by architects. It remains damaged, but intact: no one has repaired the breaks, and they in no way hinder our enjoyment of the planes and proportions.

Powerful works in the round support lacework in the form of trellises. This grey weather, this light mourning of rainy days with its washed-out ink spots all over the sky, clothes the church in a delicate haze. And the birds sing, but not the church bells. Soon, to hear the voice of church bells, shall we have to go as far as Rome?

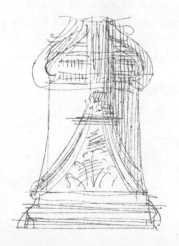

CHAPTER SEVEN

Amiens

THIS CATHEDRAL is an adorable woman, a Virgin.

What joy, what solace for the artist in finding her as beautiful as ever! Each time more beautiful! Between the Cathedral and the artist what intimate accord!

No vain confusion here, no exaggeration nor inflation. This is the absolute empire of supreme elegance.

And to think that this monument is attributed to barbaric times!

This Virgin rose here during an epoch of sincerity, to fire and perpetuate the love of beauty in men's hearts. Beneath her robe, she brought sculptors innumerable models. No, what I see here are not, or not only, saints and martyrs; they are indeed models for us. The artists of those days must have thought that in the passage of time, art would need to be brought back to truth.

I do not intend to enumerate all these models, but only certain ones that have particularly held my attention.

This angel lifting his head to show us the sky.

These two personages in prayer.

This bishop, so rich in color, dusty, patined; with his admirable head! There is a little dog, surely the artist's dog.

Nearby a man is praying within himself, without speaking; the gesture of prayer governs the beautiful folds of drapery, black only near the lower edge. The bishop lying on his tomb still speaks; a very calm precept is on his lips. Two masterpieces. This bas-relief is among the most beautiful things that exist; it has the wisdom of a Parthenon.

A Virgin places her foot on a chameleon that has a human face, slippery, slimy: superb.

A saint visits an anchorite, as beautiful as a Greek monolith of the great period.

The Angel appears to the Three Kings. Upon the large plane these figures naturally acquire an extreme majesty.

A Virgin who makes one think of Demeter.

Jesus speaks, and the men who hear him are subtle and thoughtful as so many Ulysses. They converse, one holds an owl (Wisdom), another a book (the text of the Law).

An angel gently obliges a man to lift his head—to admire the sky.

Two personages in prayer; although on their knees, they seem to be flying.

Saint John preaches in a little wood. Like Christ speaking to the people, what dramatic truth of gesture! Actors should come to study these models; they would find precious lessons.

And this beautiful Virgin in her robe with straight folds; is this not in reduced scale a symbol of the Cathedral as a whole? Those repeated folds are small columns.

In one Annunciation, the Virgin, of large stature, has an ineffable expression of condescension.

Jesus looks upon the city of Jerusalem with pity. Then he turns away, threatening. Superb bas-relief! One might take it for the enlarged obverse of a Roman coin. The gestures of pity and of anathema are almost confounded in an expression strangely complex and profoundly one.

The Pharisees have on their breast wide bands of material covered with inscriptions; on the breast, not in the heart.

What a grave, tender, and moving dialogue is exchanged between these figures twice blessed by truth and by beauty! Or rather, what harmony! Not one note of discord and no two identical notes. This is the most whole and most varied of symphonies.

And how delicious are the details that fill these bas-reliefs! Here and there, this comes from the imitation of nature, as in the clover leaves so frankly drawn, and here and there it comes from the artist's imagination, deriving no doubt still from nature, but imitating hardly more than her methods of creation.

Originality, everyone knows—and have I not already said it?—
is not in the subject, however that may seem. What is original everywhere is the consistently well-proportioned realization of a general
principle of wisdom.

The grillwork of Amiens makes perfect harmony with this
Gothic monument. Just as all beautiful things are always in accord
with each other! These Louis XIV grilles are superb in simple elegance and nobility. Sumptuously they rose at the foot of the columns.

However naïve pedants may judge an analogy between the
Gothic church and the northern forests—which were never very
far from this Cathedral and furnished it with so many materials—
that analogy imposes itself upon my mind. I am, like Chateaubriand,
absolutely convinced that the forests inspired the architect. The
builder heard the voice of nature. He understood its teaching, and
its example. He was able to deduce from them consequences of
profound and general usefulness. A tree and its shade are both the
material and the model of a house. The orderly arrangement of
trees, their varied grouping, the divisions and directions that nature
assigns to them, that is the church.

Have we not found the life of sculpture while dreaming in the
wood? Why should the architect have been less favored than the
sculptor?

And the forest still gives me an impression that is related to the one I receive from a Cathedral. Each one sends me to the other.

Both of them reawaken my youth.

So in front of this church, irresistibly I remember a forest, and I see it again.

The forest where I dreamed in my youth is severe. It has no birds. Its horizon is almost entirely closed, limited by a wall of trees. But the humid atmosphere enlivens the colors. Green lights along the sides. . .

By day this is the empire of silence, by night that of terror.

Powerful and melancholy landscape! These slashes of light . . . these ribs, these small columns . . . These Cathedral crossroads entrenched in this solitude . . . Mud hides the dead leaves from us, allowing the discovery of only a few for the sake of sharp contrast. Here are small plaques of sun; the boles of trees sliced in their plane by a sliding beam of light.

The sun is ailing, autumn sun of intermittent fires. Its rays unroll in streamers that seem to seek rest in the trees or on the ground. The sun defines and varies the melancholy charm of this late afternoon. Without it, this mood of sadness would be monotonous.

Where the horizon opens, one perceives through the trees a solemn twilight which appears to have had no beginning and never needs to end.

A little dog hesitates to follow us; we frighten him. But he is also frightened by the muddy path. Is our vanity flattered when a being smaller than ourselves fears us? I don't believe so. And yet, with respect to ourselves, we attribute that feeling to God.

In the depths there are green stained-glass windows.

A fallen tree, another; these good outstretched giants are the color of curried leather.

The path retreats. What is this brick wall? This is not a wall, but leaves against a mounting terrain.

To the right and left there open high vaulted naves that are decorated by dazzling stained glass.

My memories rise like these trees and are confounded with them.

This stern forest is the ancient forest of Soignes where I spent a few of the dreaming years of my laborious and sometimes painful youth. This forest recalls my past. A forest calls humanity back to its origins, where it retrieves its Principles.

The pulpit is of the style of Louis XVI, white and gold. And here, white and gold also, is a Louis XVI chapel. The salon is very noble with the majesty that is the mark of a time when boudoirs had nobility.

CHAPTER EIGHT

Le Mans

EACH TIME that I return here it seems to me that communication between these sublime figures and my admiration has not been interrupted. It is now twenty years and more that these figures have been my friends. The great artists who made them are my true masters. The intensity of attention with which I study them sometimes suggests the illusion that I live in those far-off days, when thought was simple, when masterpieces were the natural flowers of work.

Despite my years and this disorganized century, I return to you, patient artists, masters who are difficult to understand, and my position with regard to you is the same as that of the figures you show us leaning against the door of heaven. Their attitude tells us that they believe and that they hope. As for me, I desire, I wait with confidence the hour of comprehension, and for a long time my whole attention has been turned toward you.

The share of truth that you have revealed to me, I have used as well as I could. Perhaps I have betrayed your thought. One can express only on condition of having well understood, and in these stones there remain so many things that still escape me. All principles are here, all general laws, but it is our intelligence and our heart that are lacking or at fault. You possessed the truth, Masters, and to find it again would require more than one lifetime. Who will continue my effort when our contemporaries shall have completely shattered or obliterated these stones?

I am one of the last witnesses of a dying art. The love that inspired it is spent. The marvels of the past slip into oblivion. Nothing replaces them, and soon we shall be in night. Frenchmen are hostile to the treasures of beauty that glorify their race, and, with no one to guard these treasures, they strike them, they break them out of hatred or ignorance or by stupidity, or, under pretext of restoring, they dishonor them.

(Do not reproach me with having said this before: I should like to repeat it without ceasing so long as the evil persists!)

Alas, those marvels will not be reborn from the ashes that we make of them!

How ashamed I am for my time. How the future frightens me. With horror I ask myself what part of this crime is the responsibility of each one of us. Am I not damned along with everyone else?

And also, before what still endures of this condemned beauty, my spirit takes fright. But this fear participates in ecstasy.

The sun does not allow all to appear at once; what an admirable sight! But how mysterious it is!

My attention concentrates on these sides, so simple in their grandeur. I want to understand immediately, yet I realize that to achieve understanding I must deeply modify myself, acquire more energy, more firmness. I must submit myself to a rigorous discipline. This is difficult indeed! I project myself toward the marvel to embrace and penetrate it. But this violence repels the marvel, which demands calmness and restraint, in a word Strength, being strong in itself. And I hear the lesson. I leave but shall return. At least I carry away one sublime vision which, little by little as it ceases to astonish me, will permit me to understand.

Great emotions must take root slowly with understanding as little by little they become integral parts of the life of our sensitivity and of our intelligence. So do great trees need much time for their development. This architecture and this sculpture may truly be compared with trees, whose life out of doors they share.

Tomorrow, or perhaps later, someday, suddenly among my artist's preoccupations, the memory of my friend of stone, my Great Lady of Le Mans will return to thrill my heart and spirit, and abruptly I shall be enlightened by this clarity which, too close here, dazzles and does not allow me to rejoice in her.

But what profound and delicious commotion when at last, in a sudden illumination, I shall understand, and sense the masterpiece! A single long look overwhelms with beauty, with order, and with joy! Countless simultaneous sensations!

And this impression once acquired, I shall retain; source of enthusiasm for tomorrow, for always; a permanent miracle.

But great fatigue.

At least may my effort not be lost for others! May they inherit my admiration!

I approach slowly; already I feel the violent wind that ever blows about the Cathedrals: the Spirit bloweth.* And then I change places several times without losing sight of the details of the church. Stations of love. The profiles change but beauty is never lessened. Light and shadow play freely and strongly in these arches whose curves are so noble and so delicate!

The Masters had the modesty to give no ornament of any sort to these sixty-meter-high buttresses, straight and vertical. But I am mistaken. This is not modesty; this is wisdom and genius, *for this had to be.* This simplicity astonishes me as much, I find it as splendid,

* *Translator's note:* St. John 3:8.

as the most opulent complication of ornaments. Except at Beauvais, I know of no buttresses that thrust into the air with so much genius and measure. What simplicity! I was mistaken again: this is more than genius, this is virtue. Heroic discipline: these Masterbuilders were Roman soldiers.

And how splendid are the shadows cast by these buttresses amid this harmonious encumbrance of forest, governed by human geometry! At the summit, in a crown, the belfry triumphs, straight as a thickly planted beech grove.

Roman soldiers? No! They were giants who built this cathedral!

What a beautiful porch! There is first a gentle shadow, condensed and modeled. Nothing is hasty in this sculpture; time is needed to penetrate it. This art does not seek you, it waits for you. If you consent to come, it will teach you eternal truth. It is in no hurry.

The saints hold themselves as straight as the rule; but the rule is the principle of grace: these saints are graceful. The foliage crowns, and the halo springs up to the apex of the vault. The Christ, terrible in his gesture, the Angel, the Bull, the Lion and the Eagle: the heads are worn, broken, and yet I see them because they were in the true plane.

The plane, I have said, is everything in architecture and in sculpture. Poets, musicians, painters, is it not everything in all the arts?

These marvelous figures have no rivals except at Chartres and at Athens. What perfect understanding of bas-relief! This is the archaic Greek aspect in all its force and simplicity. The effects follow one another and complete each other by derivation. Nowhere else has the secret of life been better rendered. This is life itself, to speak more exactly. It isn't only through the hands of the artists that life is manifested. After the artists have finished, life pursues her action on their masterpieces. And these masterpieces are transformed throughout the centuries and continue to be transformed under the sun's influence, without ever having been, or ever having the possibility of becoming, inferior to themselves. On the contrary, masterpieces are more beautiful today than they have ever been, because in them the virtue of Time is added to the virtue of genius. Moreover this farsighted artist protected his figures by a projection of the architecture, a canopy which directs the light to them in oblique rays. When these rays diminish, little by little the figures enter the shadow of the canopy. But when the rays increase, every day there is the miracle of Transfiguration.

Glorious state! All returns gently, emerging from the depths. Apparitions! And the celestial conversation of heros and saints is resumed. No pure black. The four figures are as one, all enveloped in the strong softness of mingled light and shadow.

Must I change my position, move closer, and cease to see in order to examine "how this is done"? Well, in that case I must say it is done with nothing! It is never by an apparent craft that genius is revealed.

It is not by seeking to lay bare the personal secret of their genius that one overtakes the Masters; it is by following their example in the study of nature. All great artists of all times are voices singing in unison the praise of nature. Centuries may come between them; the Masters remain contemporaneous. All great moments are marked by one same and unique character: the balustrades of Blois are in the primitive Greek style.

These gowns, these skirts, these draperies are like fallen leaves.

This curving arch is made of a thousand masterpieces. Among others, this saint who glimpses heaven and whose arms, and even all her draperies, animated by desire, seek to attain it.

What beautiful cast shadows! They do not hinder the *reading* of the bodies. They make them turn and vibrate.

These capitals that burst with power, brutalized by light and shadow: only the genius of an old sculptor, a seer of yore, could bring about this miraculous result. The habit of working in the open air, at evening and at morning, with long patience and an immense love, made him all powerful.

Oh, noble race of *artisans*! So great that *artists* of today are inexistent beside you! They no longer even understand you. And yet, I do not believe the laws of light and shadow have varied or that the elements were more obedient in your time than they are today. It is we who have revolted against those laws, against the truth, and our blindness is our punishment.

The capitals of the porch are Romanesque. They are French masterpieces. What vigor in these leaves! They do not encircle, they spring up like a plant.

And the burning expression, the architectural power of these great figures at the left of the porch, seen from the entrance of the church! There is nothing more beautiful among the masterpieces of any epoch. The miracle of these *modulated blacks*!

What says this solemn-voiced bell? Is it not ringing the funeral of a king? Or the wedding march of some majestic young queen? A date is marked in my life by the intense sensation possessing me as I listen to the bell while contemplating this porch and the admirable disposition of its architecturally ordered mass of stone. Bells and sculpture speak the same great language.

How can we live without admiring these magnificent things? They fill me with gladness. My thought is strengthened in resting upon a flying buttress.

Oh, these Thousand and One Nights of intellectual delight! These celestial caryatids at the limit of simplicity. I cannot tear myself from them.

Admiration of human genius leads the spirit ever higher. As an artist, I see the Cathedrals, and I see Nature in the Cathedral.

Is it the sea breaking down there?

No, this is Vespers; I am in the church. I notice a group in prayer, and there are some people who *think*, leaning against the columns.

Te Deum! flight of archangels carrying swords! Storm, rolling of thunder!

CHAPTER NINE

Soissons at Evening

THERE IS NO TIME in this Cathedral; there is eternity. Does not Night bring it more harmony than day? Were the Cathedrals made for the night? Does not triumphant day, inundating them with clarity, too completely subdue them?

Ah, beauty of which I had foreboding! I am fully satisfied. Restorations which offended my eyes in daylight are now effaced. What an invincible impression of virginity! This flower of the catacombs is a virgin forest illuminated by powerful lights springing from one of the lateral naves.

Yes, it is at night, when all the earth is in obscurity, it is then, thanks to a few gleams, that architectures *revive*; it is then that they retrieve all their august character, as the sky regains all its grandeur during starlit nights.

Therefore I had a rendezvous last night with the image of heaven that I hold in my heart, with this heaven that shall have no morrow, perhaps. Why must this divine Cathedral be insulted? Why must this *Ecce Homo* of stone be turned to derision? And yet, during the moments that I, atom of life, spend in this Cathedral, I feel myself imbued with past centuries, the venerable centuries that produced these marvels. They are not dead! They speak in the voice of the bells! These three strokes for Angelus that sweetly strike against the sky know no obstacle or limit either in space or in time; they come to us out of the depths of the past, they rejoin our Chinese brothers and the deep vibration of the gong.

First this lordly ringing is as if the gods conversed; then it is a thrumming, like an assembly of women speaking all at one time; finally, the voice of the bell fades slowly and expires, powerful still over this gentle provincial city whose soul is a daughter of honorable simplicity, whereas Paris is the international daughter of pride.

These arcades that catch the light among shadows are in ruins. With them the spirit rests suspended in the air and in time.

In the light that strikes them, the columns are a white cloth with straight folds, the rigid folds of a sacerdotal surplice. But when they are fully lighted, they evoke parading soldiers in a respectful attitude whose straight alinement nothing will flex. And then the flame weakens, and the columns appear to be ghosts.

Exterior

In this silent square, in the immobility of night, the Cathedral has the air of a great ship at anchor.

Rain, which for centuries has poured its gusts over these stone laces, has still further whittled and perfectioned them. How far away is the time when these marvels were new! The Gothics are now as far from us as the Greeks.

All the kings of France are in this shadow, in this majestic tower that overhangs.

Day breaks. Light foregathers; it reaches the Cathedral by wide strokes, splatters the master columns, the small openwork columns, the lost profiles of the light, torus moldings. Brief half hour of delights.

CHAPTER TEN

Reims

THE CATHEDRAL is here, motionless, mute; I do not see it in the blackness of night.

As my eyes grow accustomed, I make out a little. What appears to me is the great skeleton of all the France of the Middle Ages.

This is a conscience. We cannot escape from it. It is the voice of the past.

The artists who built this Cathedral brought the world a reflection of divinity; they added their souls to ours that we might grow, and their souls belong to us. They are our soul in all the best that we have.

And we are being diminished by allowing the work of those ancient masters to perish. The artist who witnesses this crime feels himself grazed by remorse.

But the part which still remains intact retains the life of the work as a whole and defends our souls. In these ruins we have our last sanctuary. In the same way the Parthenon has defended Greece better than the shrewdest politicians could. It continues to be the living soul of a vanished people, and the least of its fragments is the Parthenon as a whole.

Seen from the three-quarters view, Reims Cathedral evokes the enlarged figure of a woman kneeling in prayer. This meaning is suggested by the form of the console.

From the same point of view, I observe that the Cathedral rises like flames.

And the richness of its profiles makes it an endlessly varied spectacle.

In studying a Cathedral, one has all the surprises, all the joys, of a beautiful journey. Such joys are infinite.

Nor do I presume to describe to you all the beauties of Reims Cathedral. Who indeed would dare to boast of having seen them all? I give only a few notes.

My aim, do not forget, is to presuade you in turn to follow this glorious itinerary: Reims, Laon, Soissons, Beauvais.

Through my open window the great voice of the bells reaches me. I listen attentively to this music, as monotonous as its friend the wind that brings it to me. I seem to hear in it at once echoes from the past, from my youth, and the answers to all the questions that I never cease to ask myself, questions which throughout my life I have sought to resolve.

The voice of the bells follows and outlines the movement of clouds; over and over it dies and is reborn, weakens, revives, and, in its immense call, the street noises, the grinding of carts and the morning cries are lost. The great maternal voice dominates the city and becomes the vibrant soul of its life. When I had ceased to listen I heard it still, and, suddenly reminded, I give it ear again; but it is beyond, it is to the people down there that the bells are speaking now. It is as if a prophet in the open air were turning this way and that way, toward the right and toward the left. The wind has changed.

But those are the centuries, and not the hours, that the bells of our great Cathedrals are tolling.

It is true that they also ring for festivals, religious festivals. Which one is for today? What a chasm that simple questions opens between the Cathedral itself and the questioner! Can anyone imagine a man of the 13th century asking, "Which festival are the bells proclaiming today?" Be interrupted ariel voices, or let your call come not so far as our ears. Let it fly away into the azure.

Suddenly I hear, "What a heap of rubbish!"

A little boy is passing with his mother close to the Cathedral and pointing to pieces of old stone carelessly stacked, old fragments of ancient sculptures that the architects have left in the workyard, all of which are masterpieces.

The young woman is delicately featured and fresh, like the statues that adorn the Cathedral. She did not reprimand the child.

From where I am, I see the radiating chapels of the apse. I glimpse this only through a curtain of old trees made bare by winter. The flying buttresses and the trees intermingle and harmonize. They are in the habit of living together. But can springtime reanimate these stones as it does those trees?

The profusion of three-storied arches in perspective makes one think of Pompeii, of those paintings where branches and arches are also blended.

I am perhaps more shocked by the restorations here than anywhere else. They date from the 19th century, and, in the fifty years since they were made, though they have gathered a patina, they deceive no one. These half-century-old ineptitudes would place themselves among the masterpieces!

All restorations are copies; this is why they are condenmed in advance. For—allow me to repeat—one must not copy with the passion of fidelity anything other than nature: the copying of works of art is forbidden by the very principle of art.

And restorations—on this point also I wish to insist again—are always soft and hard at the same time; you will recognize them by this sign. This is because science is not enough to produce beauty; there must also be conscience.

Besides, restoration involves confusion by introducing anarchy in the results. True effectiveness hides the process; to obtain true results requires much experience, long perspective, and the science of the centuries.

See, for example, the right gable of the pediment of Reims. This has not been retouched. From this powerful block emerge fragments of torsos, draperies, massive masterpieces. A simple observer, even without clearly understanding, can, if he is sensitive, experience the thrill of enthusiasm. These pieces, broken in places like those of the British Museum, are, like those also, entirely admirable. But see how the other gable, restored, remade, is dishonored. The planes no longer exist. It is heavy, worked frontally, without profiles, without equilibrium of volumes. For the Cathedral, which leans forward, this gable is an enormous weight with no counterbalancing weight. Oh, this Christ on the Cross, restored in the 19th century! The iconoclast who believed he had ruined the gable did it no great harm. But the ignorant restorer! Look again at these crawling hook-shaped leaves that have forgotten how to crawl; by such heavy restoration the equilibrium is changed.

As if it were possible to repair these figures and ornaments battered by the centuries! Such an idea could be born only in minds that are strangers to the nature of art and to all truth.

Why did you not choose the lesser of two evils? It would have been less expensive to leave these sculptures as they were. All good sculptors will tell you they find in them very beautiful models. For it is not necessary to hold to the letter, it is the spirit that matters, and this is clearly seen in these broken figures. Let your unemployed work somewhere else; they will be just as well satisfied, since it is not a certain work they are after, but the profit it brings.

They have cruelly assailed Reims. As soon as I entered, my eyes were wounded by the stained-glass windows of the nave. Needless to say they are new. Flat effects!

And these capitals, also rebuilt, representing branches and leaves; their color is uniform, flat, ineffective because the workmen held the tool frontally, at right angles to the plane of the stone. By this means one obtains only hard, unvaried results, as well say, no results. The secret of the old sculptors, on this point at least, is indeed not very complicated and would be easy to recapture. They held the tool obliquely, which is the only way to obtain modeled effects, to have slanted planes that accentuate and vary the relief.

But our contemporaries have not the least concern for variety. They do not feel it. In these capitals composed of four rows of foliage, each row is accented as much as each of the other three. Therefore the whole looks like a common wicker basket.

Whom could we convince that we are progressing? There are epochs over which taste reigns, and there are others—like this present time.

So far as a general taste is concerned, meaning a beautiful vulgarization of pure instinct, I fear this may be no more than an attribute of races in their youth; with age their sensibility becomes blunted; intelligence sags. How explain otherwise than by a weakening of the intellect the case of these pretended artists—architects, sculptors, stained glass workers—who make such restorations even while they have before their eyes the marvels that fill the Cathedrals? Their windows are in linoleum, rug windows, without depth.

The beautiful neighboring things cost the good companions of six hundred years ago less trouble. See this bouquet of flowers so French in quality!

Oh, I beg of you, in the name of our ancestors and for the sake of our children, break no more, restore no more! You who indifferently pass by, but who may understand someday and perhaps passionately, do not deprive yourself in advance and forever of this opportunity for joy, of this element of development which awaits you in this masterpiece; do not deprive your children! Consider that generations of artists, centuries of love and thought have culminated there, are expressed here. Consider that these stones signify the soul of our nation and that you will know nothing of that soul if you destroy them, that the soul will be dead, killed by you. In a single stroke you will have squandered the fortune of your country—for these are truly precious stones!

I shall not be heeded, I know it only too well. People will continue to break and to repair. Can nothing interrupt this abominable dialogue in which hypocrisy gives the cue to violence and completes the destruction of the masterpiece already mutilated by violence, while protesting that all shall be replaced by a copy, an exact repetition? Nothing can be repaired! Modern men are no more capable of producing the double of the least Gothic marvel than of repeating one of nature's marvels. A few more years of this treatment of the ailing past by the murderous present, and our bereavement will be complete and irremediable.

By our creations as well as by our restorations, does no one see where we are? Awhile ago we still understood the old styles at our Tuilleries and our Louvre museums. We stubbornly imitate them even today, but how!

The belfries of Laon and of Reims are brothers or sisters.

How each one perpetually recalls the other, and yet what variety between the Cathedrals! How numerous are the Cathedrals, and how unique each one is! Variety in unity; one must not tire of repeating those words. The day when they are completely forgotten, nothing in the French world will be in its place.

It is analogy that binds things and assigns them to their ranks. This tower of Reims is a psalm. This tower: it could be interrupted or continued. What matter, since its beauty is in the modeling?

The Portal.

These figures of bishops are truly capable of hurling lightning; these humble servants who hold the Book; this great majestic figure of a woman, the Law.

The admirable figure of Saint Denis* on the north portal carries his head in his hand, and two angels, at the place where his head should be, hold a crown. May I see a symbol here? It is this: ideas, cut off, interrupted in their unfolding development, shall be recovered, shall reign later, in a day that shall have no ending.

* *Translator's note:* This figure carrying his head is on the north transept portal, *Portail St. Sixte.* It portrays St. Nicaise, not St. Denis. Opposite on the same transept portal is an inferior portrait of St. Denis with his head on his shoulders, a late work.

The Virgin on the pier,* whose face is illumined, is a true woman of France, of the French provinces, a beautiful plant of our garden.

Perfect sculpture of wise, skillful oppositions. The large folds of the cloak of state leave the delicious breast and head in light.

The pier column is adorned with small salient figures. If the details are not Greek, the planes are, and these determine and uphold the general beauty of the composition.

Tapestries of Reims.

These admirable designs, these colors that are as reserved as those of frescoes, this touching story of the Virgin: does not all this bring the soul to flower? And is this not the state of mind that the artist wished to produce? All the backgrounds and the intervals are filled with tiny flowers which, in the tapestry, are fastened to nothing, except to our souls.

These tapestries are works of a supreme art.

And this art belongs to us! The Egyptians, the Greeks—at least so I believe—did not have such works as these tapestries, woven with multicolored grains of dust, the dust of our past! They are like prim-

* *Translator's note:* A pier is an isolated mass of masonry, a large column, like those between the nave and its aisles, as distinguished from the more slender columns.

itive frescoes, Japanese prints, and Chinese vases: in them all is fore-seen.

What luxury! And what wisdom in luxury!

Silver-grey enhanced with blue, with red, and still the tapestry matches the stone; it is the color of incense.

One need not know the subject of the composition to judge its beauty. Here Measure reigns; this is its empire, this its throne. But the subjects too, in themselves, contribute an element of beauty of which the embroiderer was admirably able to take advantage.

Here is the presentation of Jesus to Simeon: how beautiful the Virgin's draperies are! This is the Adoration of the Magi: how well this relief expresses majesty in these royal figures! Next is the Flight into Egypt where the Virgin on an ass is accompanied by angels that are as graceful as those of Botticelli. Here is the Massacre of the Holy Innocents. All these compositions are divided and dis-tributed according to the order of a Pompeian architecture. One feels that he is leafing through a book of hours of incomparable splendor. Perfect full-length portraits complete these *Stanze* of another Vatican. I see again a portrait of a prophet speaking to the multitudes. He affirms, he evangelizes.

A suave grey harmonizes all these tapestries. To their long stay in this Cathedral which they illumine, they owe their hue of the cen-turies. This thread has the same age as this stone. And those who placed here stone upon stone and stitch upon stitch are collaborators in a single task. The textile and the mineral join together, unite, and are prolonged in love with each other.

Dead leaf heightened in tone; diamond dust; encrusted wheat cockles of a beautiful cherry red; these adorable tones have lived together, are molten, and their union today constitutes I know not what of an unparalleled richness and splendor.

And the draperies, by the style of their folds, make one think of Holbein.

David's gable also has been repaired. Now there is nothing to see. The old gable was visible from below; the new one doesn't give that effect. One feels that the worn-out spirit could not attain to expression, and this insignificant David is there in place of the original one. It makes no contact with the gaze that rises from beneath.

Romanesque Portal

The restored part of the door is ruined, lost. The body of the door, despite its wounds, retains all its youthfulness. In place of the molding, since that has disappeared, deeply cut ovolos and darts are substituted.

Statue in the Royal Square.

The statue of Louis XV at Reims is a noble example of the best arrangement. There are fortunate blacks where the figures rest on the pedestal, and the statue itself is admirable in wisdom, irreproachable in its planes; and, besides the beauty of the figures, is that of the tablet, so easily and happily accomplished! Ignorant people, and even some connoisseurs, weary of this sumptuousness, have scoffed at this beautiful work. They are like the bourgeois of the time of Louis Phillippe who presume to give a lesson to the contemporaries of Louis XV.

Portrait* of Saint Remi.

This figure is corroded by the centuries, yet the centuries have not reached what is most precious in its beauty, they have respected the large volumes. And just as it is here, this figure is still the friend of time, and of all times.

It is the sister of those beautiful Greek fragments of which I have seen plaster casts whose first and second layer of marble, worn, effaced, or destroyed, seem lifted away. From this you expect to find the plane somewhat deteriorated. But it remains visible to him who knows how to look for it, since the plane is the volume itself. Time

* *Translator's note:* The French word here is *portail*, but there is no portal of St. Remi at Reims. The subject of this page is the beautiful portrait of St. Remi at the left angle of the north portal on the principal west façade of the cathedral. See E. Moreau-Nelaton, "La Cathédrale de Reims," *Beaux Arts*, 1915, p. 105, planch 52.

can do no harm to planes that are true. It only harms the ill-made figures. They are lost as soon as they are touched; wear, from the first stroke, uncovers the falsehood. But a figure that is admirable as it comes from the artist's hands remains admirable however ravaged it may be. The work of bad artists has no duration because essentially it never has existed.

This handsome monument shows all the reasoned and measured power of style.

I always come back to this word "discipline" to define this sober and strong architecture. It reassures and satisfies me. What absolute knowledge of proportions! Only the planes count, and everything is sacrificed to them; this is wisdom itself. Here I reaffirm my soul with something solid that is my own; for I am an artist, and I am a plebeian and Cathedrals were made by artists for the people.

In a particularly imperious way, the sensation of style awakes in me this idea of quiet possession.

The sensation of style. How far it leads! By an obscure route, thought remounts or redescends as far as the catacombs, as far as the source of this great river: French architecture.

For a very long while it was agreed that the art of the Middle Ages was nonexistent. It was—let us tirelessly repeat in order to silence that insult which throughout three centuries was ceaselessly aimed at it—"barbarism." Even today the most daring minds, those that boast of understanding Gothic art, still have reservations. But this art is one of the majestic sides of beauty.

May the word *powerful* be taken here in its fullest meaning: this art is very *powerful!* I think of Rome, of London. I think of Michelangelo. This art gives France a severe countenance. Only too much time has been lost in seeking an accord between weakness and beauty —"the ideal" of today!

I · THE CATHEDRAL AT NIGHT · DISTANT GLEAMS turn brown and blacken before certain columns. They clarify others obliquely, feebly yet regularly.

But the depth of the chancel and the whole left part of the nave are plunged in a thick gloom. The effect is horrible because of the indecision of things in the lighted distance. A whole square space is struck by stark illumination; lights flame between columns that take on colossal proportions. And I am made to doubt this epoch and this country by the interruptions, these conflicts of light and shadow, these four opaque columns before me and these six others lighted farther off on the same oblique line, and then by the night in which I am bathed and which submerges everything. There is no softness. I have the impression of being in an immense cavern from which Apollo will arise.

STUDY · 175

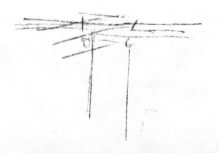

176 · LOCHES

LOUDUN · 177

178 · STUDY

AUXERRE · 181

182 · VETHEUIL

For a very long while I cannot define the horrible vision. I no longer recognize my religion, my Cathedral. This is the horror of the ancient mysteries. At least so I should suppose if I no longer felt the architectural symmetry. The vaulted ceilings are barely perceptible, braced by shadows, the ribs of the arches.

I must escape the oppression of this effect *of closing in*. A guide takes me by the hand, and I move through darkness that soars as far as the vault.

From the light beyond them, these five columns have their oblique illumination. The ribs, the arched ceiling beams, the ogives resemble crossed flags, like those at the Invalides.

I advance. It is an enchanted forest. The tops of the five columns are no longer visible. The pale lights that cross the balustrades horizontally create infernal roundelays.* Here one is in heaven by day, and in hell by night. Like Dante, we have descended into hell.

Violent contrasts are like those from torchlight. Ardent fire at the mouth of a tunnel spreads out in layers. Only the columns against this flaming background are indistinctly black. At moments a drapery appears with a red cross; the light seems to be extinguished, but, no, it persists in a mortal immobility.

*Translator's note: dances in the round. See Albert E. Elsen, *Rodin*, Museum of Modern Art, New York, 1963, pp. 155–156.

The chancel is laid bare to horror. But the horror controls itself, imposes order, and this order reassures us. And then, our memory of day, our connections with the day come at this moment to our rescue, giving us the necessary confidence.

There is a reflection on one ogive; the perspective is masked and the clarity, imperfectly developed on the edge, shows only the stationary construction in the dim gleam. But this gleam, although terrible, nevertheless reveals the masterpiece.

The Cathedral assumes an Assyrian character. Egypt is vanquished, for this Cathedral is more poignant than the Pyramid, farther from us than the grottos where the great creation of rules appeared. The unknown is the mystery of this spectacle. One thinks of a forest, of a grotto, but this is nothing of that sort: this is something absolutely new, which it is impossible to define at once.

The frightful bulk of night, feebly pushed aside for a moment, as quickly, and with an irresistible violence, regains empire.

This is like Rembrandt, but *as a spectre of taste and of order.* Rembrandt himself brings us not more than an echo of this prodigious world.

I am in terror and in rapture.

Dante, did you enter this circle of horror?

The chapels are transformed by the struggle between darkness and light.

This one is a somber grotto where there seem to be only shells set out along the ribs of the arches. And yet, the terrible shadow allows itself to be seen, appreciated, and modeled.

Another chapel is divided in two by a cast shadow. One whole side is abolished. The columns seen from three-quarters, black and formidable, disturb the whole architectural arrangement. My dissipated mind apprehends only frightful things; it sees horrible supporting legs repeated in this forest that man has created for his God. Is this forest less beautiful than the real one? Is it animated by fewer thoughts, less populated by atrocious larvi and by fewer spirits?

And you, gargoyles, did you not issue from the brain of sculptors who returned to the Cathedral after sunset to take counsel there from night and to seek there the memory of some horrible dream?

I aspire to a new confirmation of the grandeurs of the Gothic soul.

One would have the impression of a Tower of Babel if, in this apparent confusion, all at once architectures did not surge out of the night, if the shadow itself were not organized. The moment is present without words and without voice.

Completely black columns are around the chancel; this is stone in prayer, a waterspout that rises to God.

Oh Night, you are greater here than anywhere else. It is because of the half illumination that terror comes over me. Incomplete illuminations cut the monument into trunks, and these gleams tell me the thrilling pride of the Titans who built this Cathedral. Did they pray? Or did they create?

Oh genius of man, I implore you, remain with us, god of all reflections!

We have seen what the human eye had not yet seen, what is perhaps forbidden it to see. Orpheus and Eurydice feared being unable to escape, since the boatmen did not come to fetch them in the terrible gloom. We walked alone amid Night. We were in the straits of Tarn. We went alone into a great forest. A whole world was in this Night that the Titans had prepared for us.

A candle burns: a tiny point of light. To reach it I must stride over heavy masses of shadow where I rub against dead gleams, unicorns, monsters, visions.

The *Thinker** would have been well adapted to this crypt; this immense shadow would have fortified that work.

By lighting a candle, the sacristan has displaced the shadows.

* *Translator's note:* This refers to Rodin's enlarged figure of the *Thinker*.

There is a treasure here, the treasure of shadow accumulated by night. It hides the treasure of the Cathedral.*

As we reached the door, this gigantic scene advanced toward us: the immense room seemed prepared for a banquet to the infernal gods.

Then the small door of the Cathedral was closed. The vision disappeared. All is entrusted now to our memory.

II · *From my window.*

Before making my way toward the Cathedral to pay it one more nocturnal visit, I contemplate it from the window of this room which I have chosen because it is very close to the colossal wonder.

Constructions charged with thought! Accumulation of thoughts over this façade, this bas-relief of which from my window I see but one part. What race of men made this? Thousands of years, centuries have their portrait here. This is a visage of human infinity.

Inside the Cathedral.

From the depths of the nave, from the chancel as a whole, one

* *Translator's note:* The French word here is *église* (Church), but obviously it refers to the Cathedral of Reims.

feels repulsed by shadow out of which, hollow and confused, come terrifying forms. And I believe I hear an irritated voice reprimanding me:

"Who dares to invade my solitude? Am I not the Virgin of Night? Are these shades no longer my own? Who dares to enter here?"

I felt that I violated the rights of silence, that a sacrilegious hand opened to me the heart of this holy silence. But an artist is able to understand, and he is not a profane outsider here.

Everywhere one feels unalterable foundations. All is security. The pillars are certitudes. This is admiration transfixed, congealed into lordly columns all alined like an army.

The pillars, reassuring in all their dimensions, are more real the closer they are to the ground. There are effects of light on the stone pavements. The small columns appear to be pleated.

Other columns are like trees that uphold the vault and the sky, that lift the antique night. Again they force upon me the image of ranks of disciplined soldiers. They are bordered with light. They stand erect like a wood; their type is a beech wood. Above, one sees only the design of their branches. Silence accompanies their moldings as far as the pinnacle, the silence of immobility, for the wind here causes nothing to move, and these trees are indoor plants. Along the height of these columns, of these trees, feeble gleams mount which will be lost in the shadow of the vault. In their lightness, the ribs appear as lofty spiderwebs.

In short, these pillars set out in an arc, directly support nothing but shadow, only black clouds. Starting from the feebly lighted base, their shafts terminate in the unknown. And yet, the ceiling restores truth up there, which the shadows uphold. I have above my head an abyss of height, but an abyss so well ordered that illusion harmoniously shifts its emphasis when the lights move.

This Renaissance pillar is not completely lost in that abyss. It grows spindle shaped in rising and is delicately enclosed in the somber cloud. One feels that high up there, above black rocks, fire birds furiously beat their wings; there is a struggle, and from that conflict of forces, order is born.

I am at the heart of a pyramid.

How strange that a tiny candle flame should be able, as it vacillates, to make the monster palpitate, should move architectures which at this moment are immobile! A slight variation of light, and all this will move.

Short prelude; a peal: voice of the minute.

This chant, up there, is like a warning for the angels; in the half-light, time immemorial is about to ring.

The bell, sound of forges, the swinging of small bells pour vibrations over all.

From my window.

Looking again at the Cathedral through my window, I see a curtain of stone whose sculptures are its embroideries. Faust would deserve the privilege of living in this room, by this window, in the shadow of the portal of the masterpiece whose splendor exalts this street, this city, this country.

The immense bas-relief is still there in the darkness; I cannot distinguish it but I feel it. Its beauty persists and, triumphing over shadow, allows me to admire its powerful black harmony. The bas-relief overbrims the bay of my window almost hiding the sky.

How explain that the Cathedral, even wrapped in veils of night, loses nothing of its beauty? Can the power of this beauty possess us beyond our senses? Does the eye see without sight? Is this prestige due to the virtue of the monument, to the merit of its immortal presence, its tranquil splendor? A marvel acts upon the sensibility beyond the restricted domain of a particular organ, thanks to the intervention of memory. A few reference points are sufficient, and the alerted mind, accepting the work's legitimate authority, opens to its sublime influence and recognizes, despite imprecision, the regularity of the general form. And yet the mind does not succeed in deciphering all. It awaits revelation.

ANOTHER VIEW OF THE CATHEDRAL · I WALK in remotest antiquity.

Below, a small light outlines a crown, and the columns seem the columns of Night.

A light carried by the sacristan penetrates the gloom like a ploughshare driven through clods of earth. Light bears down, and the shadow quivers to the left and right; it passes, and the blocks of shadow close again over this gleaming furrow.

Above are crumbling stalactites of shadow! These fall into a swamp of shadow which itself augments in contrast to the light. One seems to walk in a forest at night beneath trees of winter. Glimmers accumulate in the between-columns, drawing curves that transect each other, and yet one remains lost in obscurity. I repeat that, if one did not hold onto the feeling for order amid perspectives sketched by the errant light, fear would be invincible.

The top of the monument is marked by long grey streaks. At the base, gleams filter through. And for all my struggle, I discover nothing. I bang against the impassive wall, the sublime wall where no detail appears, which all the same gives me the sensation of modeling. Morning, the revealer, when the monster sleeps no more, will tell us what veils, what triple veils, hid from us the sight whose splendor I divined. For the moment I owe as much to my imagination as to my eyes. I stand before an impenetrable mask.

The small light that moves, step by step, evokes the idea of a crime. In this way a dim lantern would accompany the steps of a criminal.

Man's genius triumphs in the creation of arcades. From where did this idea come? From the rainbow perhaps?

Transept.
I seem to see the staircase of Chambord developed to vast proportions. Spirals pass into the heights, bridges are outlined whose bases plunge into the shadow of the transept cross.

These great roses, the stained-glass windows, these suns by day, are by night more black than all the other parts of the Cathedral.
The chapels are the alveolus cells of a beehive.

Shadow flattens the pilasters. Here and there are streaks less black. One distinguishes graduated forms which the confused light masks without regularity, especially when I look from the three-quarters view. The imposing richness of grey and black remains.

Purity and lightness result from this: that the prismatic form always lights masses by a sharp edge.

Exterior of the Cathedral by day.

Through the open doors, above the white columns springing toward the vault, the stained-glass windows on bright days are Persian images. And the group of columns, seen beneath the arcades and the vaults, seem pushed away by the back windows.

From my room, all bathed in shadow cast by the Cathedral, I see from my bed the vast bas-relief; this is one part of the façade. And my whole room, like my thought, is engulfed in this work which draws me. I think of the thousands of men who have worked at *that*.

Very few living today pay homage to this desert of divine stones that were formerly so much admired. I come to them, led by the love that defends us both from death. I feel I am the sundial's needle, continuing to mark the vital and glorious hours upon the dial of humiliated centuries.

What friendly breeze refreshes my brow? It is the wind that has just touched the Cathedral. Hardly any others than the wind and I have remained faithful.

Weary, I had started back toward my room and was taking, nevertheless, one hundred steps before going in; the sun stretched its rays to infinity, and all at once the Cathedral *allowed itself to be seen!* The marvel of marvels had waited for me to brim my heart, my soul, and brain with its splendor, to strike me with its divine lightning and its magnificent thunder. I was alone before the colossus. Moments at once of annihilation and of extraordinary life! Sublime apotheosis! Sacred terror! Unexpectedly, light reveals the unexpected.

Things appeared to me more lofty, purified. They faded to nothing, transformed by glory. Lights that emphasized the first planes were interrupted to take more power in following the ascendant lines, leaving the porches to fill with mist, to be dissolved in shadow, while beyond, the Cathedral thrust its audacious framework to heaven.

Exterior of the Cathedral at night.

These guardians of shadow over the door forever, these great witnesses, this guard of honor in three ranks—by four, by six, by ten—these saints seem to be resuscitated souls standing in their tombs.

Throbbing about these strange figures, I feel a soul that is not from among us. What a terrible enigma they are to me! They seem to be bearing witness, they live the life of the centuries. Are they apparitions? They have a formidable religious intensity. Do they not of one accord await some grave event? They are no longer of the time of their carving. Their aspect constantly changes, and for me these figures have a singularly new and foreign accent. I think of Hindustan, of Cambodia.

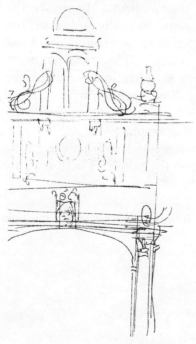

CHAPTER ELEVEN

Laon

I HAVE PREFACED this charming journey by a visit to the Louvre.

Once again I have established to the point of evidence how much the Greeks sought color at the same time as form. Moreover, it is certain that, when well rendered, form expresses color and *vice versa*.

Thus the antique palm-leaf motif, beside these shallow basins and this victory, derive from the same principle. The great sculptors, not satisfied with expressing themselves powerfully through planes, were guided by their infallible taste to draw attention where needed by a dark accent, a black shadow, a stroke of emphasis wisely placed.

But what moderation in the use of that emphasis!

In our time, points of emphasis are so squandered that there is no one effect which harmoniously governs the whole. There are only vain violences that confess weakness.

Measure is lost, that Greek virtue which is the sign of conscious power.

Measure was also first among all characteristically French virtues during the beautiful times of the Romanesque, Gothic, Renaissance, and all that followed as far as the time of Louis XVI.

In my profound admiration before this porch, I feel surrounded by glory.

The three towers of Laon, seen at a distance, are like flags that carry abroad the just pride of man.

From the moment of entering this Cathedral what preparation! Children coming for their First Communion, in their white dresses and white veils, gather under the porch. How many things to admire at once! The varied beauty of all this youth and the sublime ordering of the Cathedral.

The ceremony is already beginning. My gaze that wandered into one of the small chapels is distracted by the rhythmical action, graceful and harmonious, of the celebrants in rich costumes and by this white-clad congregation of the young faithful.

Soul of France, I find you again! Here I experience the same sense of true restraint in its free and living expansion that I recognized at the Louvre in the immobility of the Antique.

What sacred objects these women are! What natural decoration they are to this forest of stone! How all in them, types, attitudes, clothing, adapts to the style of the building, enters with ease and maintains itself in this atmosphere!

Yes, the Greeks were right to say that beauty is virtue. This calm beauty, the enemy of all violence, grave and restrained, which they loved and which they transmitted to us, is beauty that conceals its strength beneath the delicate veil of grace.

That grace, theirs and ours, is the supple, agile, and easy gesture of vigor, of energy, animating, even to this day and among us, all that is not yet irremediably weary or vanquished. These young girls, these young women that surround me, do not know they are perfect models of grace.

Oh, sacred charm of true womanhood of which the great city is oblivious!

I come back to the small chapels that I love so much, these small and varied Renaissance chapels that circle around the whole interior of the Cathedral.

Here I breathe a subtle spirit, the aroma of this stone flower. Its so-varied beauty permits comparison with the most beautiful Greek works. What delicious compositions!

Was there perhaps competition among you, companions? And what were your names? Brunelleschi, or Donatello, or Ghiberti? At least you were not their inferiors. As for me, I find you even more intense, less cold, than the great Italians. And yet God knows that I love them!

How I wish I might summon my friends, and everyone, to this place to share all the joy that I feel! But no one will have it. It is for me, for myself absolutely alone—so it seems to me. How these masterpieces must weep over their ruin, prepared and assured by the criminal masters of our so-called civilization.

Oh France, land where Apollo took refuge and, still divine, is it possible that you should have fallen into this barbarism smitten with death? This barbarism is pleased to destroy beauty or to deprave it, to discuss, to question, and cast doubt upon man's genius and its works, these treasures of generations, the splendor of nature, and the splendor also of its human interpretation!

Falsehood, worse than death, has been working here at death's side. And the silence of the sanctuary has lost its real meaning now that its stained-glass windows are replaced. These columns are now no more than banal masonry, bearing nothing but wounds. These wounds still have their beauty, they tell a dolorous and heroic tale. But the new barbarians do not see these stigmata; they would not understand them if it occurred to them to look. They cry out, they strike, they destroy. Or they efface, they change, they betray. And the people do not protest.

Prayer is no longer at home among these desecrated stones.

How harmoniously the human voice resounds in this Cathedral! Two workmen in a corner speak of their work: there is a grandeur as of words enhanced in value.

The pediment of Laon is a bas-relief of the Virgin. Admirable sculptural composition.

The angels come to fetch the Virgin. The impression is of a snowy purity; they waken her. Two of them have thuribles. This is the sentient resurrection.

The Last Judgment.

The Apostles are seated at the right and left of Christ, who forms the keystone of the vault.

What a span this vault has! Saint Sebastian lifts his arm to its highest point.

The vaulting surfaces are birds' wings.

I have looked at this vault for a long time, and I no longer feel tired. It seems to me that I also have wings.

What joy to feel in my little hotel room that I am only two steps away from the marvel, this mute giant, protector of the city!

Such monuments are the great trees of the human forest. Centuries have consolidated them. But the human ax is at their base also, as at the trunks of other trees that beget beautiful landscapes.

Oh, I am feverish to see it again. My mind might forget; I need to understand it again.

The Cathedral of Laon is more than half dead.

And yet, what one still sees of it surpasses the powers of admiration. What decision in variety! What an extraordinarily precise sense of effectiveness!

Rabelais, du Bellay, Ronsard (I think of the little Renaissance chapels) did you make the plans for these chapels? Or was the architect your brother? (I say Ronsard here; I do not say Racine.)

Oh marvels, even now I mourn for you, even now while you still exist. Who knows? Perhaps you will revive.

All returns, is reestablished or reconstituted during the course of time. Therefore the hour must indeed sound when artists will assume the great task of returning to the Spirit its despoiled domain. But it was necessary that someone should take the initiative to point out this duty.

I am the forerunner. Yes, I understand; another will come!

Oh happiness! But who? And may I not unloose the lachet of his shoes?* Is it not time? For these stones are at the point of death.

* *Translator's note:* St. Luke 3:16.

Let us make haste to save their souls within ourselves. Artists, is this not our duty? Is it not in our own interest and the only means of defending ourselves against barbarism?

Let us love, let us admire! Let us make sure that those about us love and admire. If the work of the giants who constructed these venerable buildings must disappear, let us make haste to hear the lesson of those great masters. Let us read it in this work and strive to understand so that neither we, nor those whom we love better than ourselves, our children, may be reduced to despair when this work shall indeed be lost. Divine nature will outlive that destruction and continue to speak the great language these masters heard which they have magnificently translated for us here. Spare us the sorrow and the shame of realizing too late that we in our time might have understood Them had we listened to THEM.

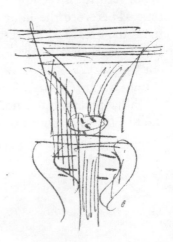

CHAPTER TWELVE

Chartres

(Notes made at various dates.) · I · My DAY shall not be lost!

The train races. Long ribbons of road, of fields, yellow, green, and chocolate brown, all descend before our course and beneath the immutable sky.

It is to Chartres that we are going.

I have very often visited this Cathedral, but today it appeared entirely new to me, more beautiful, more brilliant than ever, and I began to study it as if I were seeing it for the first time.

Chartres has become a hymn of praise for eternity.

Chartres, our Cathedral, splendid among all others!

Is it not the Acropolis of France?

Palace of Silence. The crowds fill it; groups come and go through its portals, in its naves, continually climbing and descending the steps of its towers, and for centuries that has been so. But this ancient movement that will not cease, has in no way interrupted its silence. This is because, when faced by a marvel, one is hushed by a happiness obscurely perceived, or by an admiration that surpasses words.

Day and night embellish it equally though differently. The first awakens a delicate grace; the second a terrible majesty.

Oh, how the cultivated and weary minds of our time are astonished to find so close to the centers of modern agitation this calm and sublime summary of centuries devoted to the research and accomplishment of beauty! As at every other place, one may come to pray to God at Chartres since He is everywhere. But one may come here also to contemplate man, who is revealed here in his genius and who, in that aspect, is not everywhere.

At Chartres our ancestors realized their masterwork during a time when the genius of the race knew an all-powerful period comparable to the one Greece knew during its apotheosis.

Frail shadows of those who were before us, we come to slake our thirst at the springs that gushed from their genius and their faith; sources of light! To understand, to love this incomparable epic is to increase. It is by a supernatural light that we are enlightened here.

II · THE CATHEDRAL is surrounded by faithful and powerful friends who uphold it in its attitude of prayer as the Hebrews held Moses' arms extended up toward God. These friends are the buttresses, giants sixteen meters tall, blond at the base and more and more dark as they approach the roofing. Their presence, their assistance, contribute singularly to the general effect of meditative power which the whole monument creates.

And from the bases of these buttresses, from the foundations of the famous belfry, delicate ornaments spring up and thicken as if gathering momentum within themselves to carry their flight still higher; and soon there is a whole flowering.

How powerful and stocky, like a ship's staircase, are the buttresses of the nave in contrast to those of the belfry!

These buttresses have at the top a small niche where a figure bathes in shadow.

All the planes are in half-tone. Power is reserved for the black which, without thinness, encircles the large figures.

Architectural lines are the only ones that count in the sculptured figures of Chartres. The instinct of the artists of genius who worked in this Cathedral taught them that the human body projects architecturally or, to say that better, it generates architecture by the same token as the trees and the mountains.

How true, simple, and grand are the gestures of these figures! They incline the head forward in curiosity and submission, both at once. Free human gestures are always beautiful. But the gestures of these statues, repeated during so many centuries, have acquired I know not what sacred character of slow majesty.

And yet . . . Thirty years ago I saw the right lateral portal for the first time. How many changes since then! I no longer find that suppleness, that delicious envelope, thanks to which these sculptures appeared as if veiled in morning mist which allowed only the outstanding features to be seen. I can no longer find the atmosphere created by true artists.

Alas, this has disappeared beneath successive restorations, all of which are equally to be condemned.

But I have just had a vision upon which I close my eyes, trying to retain it always. Among the sculptures of the left portal, this woman, this older man — what superhuman knowledge of the Plane!

Is it not precisely this science, this science of sciences, this unique science, this principle of *architectural sculpture*, that is most lacking in our epoch?

In this beautiful weather, I see in all their sharpness these sober profiles at once expanded by eloquence and compressed almost to straight lines. What audacity! This always astonishes me. We have so acquired the habit of neglecting the principal matter that its expression has become incomprehensible.

Oh, the beauty of the vaulting surfaces! Only at this moment I notice them, and here for three days I have studied, I have admired. But I am a little dazzled by so much splendor.

Why did I not go to school here, with these vaulting surfaces! It is true that earlier I might not have understood them. Is not this understanding the result, or fruit, of the efforts of my whole life that I gather at this time when my admirations are founded on such solid certainties? May my example have a measure of authority among the true lovers of Beauty.

Glorious authors of the Parthenon, acknowledge here the work of your brothers, of your equals. Concerning the great science of sculpture in the open air, the Gothics knew as much as you.

And I—if I may be permitted a personal reflection—have I not walked in your footsteps as well as in theirs? Did I not approach you a little, Greek masters, Gothic masters, through my statue of Balzac, which, whatever one may say of it, is nonetheless a decisive step for sculpture in the open air?

The secret of the Gothic! Let us strive to understand the Greeks;

if we succeed in that, we shall have but few efforts to make to understand our twelfth and thirteenth centuries.

Austere and rewarding studies! With what enthusiasm I pursue them! Today I have the reward of so many years of obstinate work.

I enter.
At first the extreme dazzlement allows me to perceive only luminous purples; then little by little I distinguish an immense arcade, a sort of ogival rainbow which appears near the ressaut of the pillars.
The mystery fades slowly. Slowly the architecture becomes precise, and admiration is irresistibly affirmed.

III · WHAT ALWAYS MOVES ME most profoundly in this Cathedral, is the sense of wisdom it imposes upon me.
Chartres is wise with an intense passion.
A feat of invention and of work. Palace of peace and of silence.
The great vault of pale shadow is upheld at the points where it falls back by columns between which there darkens a hard, raw black, destined to preserve the vault at once from all heaviness and from all flabbiness.
Here an heroic peace reigns.
And the Cathedral as a whole is composed with such knowledge

of harmony that each one of the elements of the composition gives to all the others a formidable reverberation. In the buttresses, for example, there is beauty of contrast: thick-set buttresses contrast with delicate slender moldings; repose pervades wherever it is possible to favor the suave effect of the flowering above and the animation concentrated at the doors.

This very animation is measured, controlled, dictated by the requirements of the monument and by its destination.

This morning, a procession of young girls preceded me. I seem to see the Cathedral statues move and breathe. They came down from the walls to kneel in the nave. What an air of kinship between those figures and these children! In both is the same blood. The sculptors of Chartres had long observed the features and the physiognomy of their contemporaries, the countenance, the bearing of these simple and beautiful creatures whose relaxed and modest movements have so much natural style! They pass, discrete, showing but little of their beauty in the mystery which the rites require, without, however, being able to hide all from an artist. Those sculptors knew how to see such beauty. They studied, understood, and loved it. Nature, which, in its essential elements has not varied despite the centuries from the 13th to our own, testifies to the sincerity of those great observers. They copied the sweet nature of this land. They reproduced the grace which, from full hands, God distributed over the countenances of the women of their time, as over those of our own time. The stone saints who tell us their ancient sorrows and hopes belong to this corner of France and to today.

What belongs only to today, alas, is the folly of restoration. That work of the Pharisees troubles my joy; my eyes, given to admiring, in quest of new motives for admiration, are suddenly stricken.

These Pharisees proceed from the letter, which kills. They say, "You see, we operate according to the best receipts . . ." Receipts that are indeed infallible—for destroying. They have killed certain of the stained-glass windows that were among the most precious motives of the glory of Chartres. They have killed the pilasters which even in summer, even at midday, are no longer seen because the nature and economy of the light have been changed.

How can one fail to understand that the Gothics, in modeling light and shadow as they did, knew what they wanted and how they could realize their desire? How can any doubt that they were obedient at once to an absolute science of harmony, and to irresistible necessities? Why is the current bad taste not content with the ugliness it produces? Why, on top of that, does it insult the past and deprive us of the share of happiness which the Cathedral had dedicated to us for always? See at Chartres what a delicious introduction is prepared for us in the marvelous stories told by the sculptures and ornaments of the portals. These are scenes that unroll one from the other like the fantasies of a very clear and very delicate dream. But the hideously low-relief restorations that intrude are no more than hard and dry repairs. The very feeling for sculpture in the round, which is so sweet and essentially appropriate to the style, which is the very soul of this style, is lacking in the authors of these repairs; perhaps it is lost.

IV · I AM ALWAYS ASTONISHED by the presence at Chartres of those Renaissance pilasters with the lovely symmetrical ornaments which, from top to bottom, outline such graceful arabesques.

Ribbons that unroll, perfume burners, birds whose necks are immeasurably elongated and which bend to forage among the leaves and fruit; other birds, that recall the phoenix, drink flames from horns of abundance. Foliage falling in a plumb line marks the line which connects this frail arabesque with the whole length of the composition. In all centers, are tablets filled with inscriptions. On the sides are symbolic lizards and birds like those seen everywhere since Romanesque times. Again, on the sides are scrolls of flower pattern. And satyrs escaping from vases to encircle women and children with their arms, and adorable sirens enveloped in leaves to their thighs, and angels that amuse themselves by spanking little satyrs. And these two other satyrs with faces lifted high carrying candlesticks in their outspread arms, and still another satyr who carries a whole dinner service on his head.

The authors of these little marvels were pupils of Rabelais or of his emulators.

V · RELIGIOUS MUSIC, twin sister of this architecture, completes the flowering of my soul and my intelligence. Then it grows silent; but for a long while still it vibrates within me, helping me to penetrate to the profound life of all this beauty which never ceases to be renewed and transformed according to the points from which one contemplates it. Move a meter or two, and all changes; yet the general order persists, as in the varied unity of a beautiful day. The Gregorian antiphons and responses have also this character of unique and diverse grandeur; they modulate silence as Gothic art models shadow.

What fearsome and sweet magnificence!

Never have I felt so keenly the grandeur of man's genius. I feel myself grow as a result of this flood of admiration. In this way a people might be reborn who would take the trouble to look, who would seek to understand. So without respite I cry to my own: there is nothing so beautiful to see, nothing so *useful* to study as our French Cathedrals and, above all, this one! Why have you become blind, heirs of the visionaries who accomplished this masterpiece?

Now music, confusedly heard awhile ago, grows precise and ordered. Charmed from age to age, the joy of innumerable souls wells up from this Cathedral, which itself is music, and these are like two harmonies that pursue one another, that meet and lovingly melt together. Life launches out from the shadow and mounts to the pinnacle in luminous and melodious spirals. I apprehend angels' voices.

What words could express the happiness that is bestowed upon me from all sides, this entranced astonishment of a soul that feels itself suddenly winged within the hued and singing shadow?

This dust of light, this scintillation of shadow, that Rembrandt taught us to admire, did he not borrow it from you, Cathedrals? He alone knew by another art how to express, how to define the miracle by transposing the inexhaustible opulence of these modeled shadows.

VI · WHAT IS this archaic line?

The Angel! the Angel of Chartres!

I walk around this figure. I study it but not for the first time and, as always, with insistence.

I will to understand!

And hours have passed. I leave exhausted by my efforts, and I am anxious.

But at evening I return. I admire, and it seems that I shall be better able to clarify the motives of my admiration now that there is no sun on the Angel. I am willing, like a good workman; my task is to understand, and I assemble all my powers to this end. I contemplate.

And always the miracle dazzles me. This self-respect! This nobility! The Angel of Chartres is like a bird perched at the angle of some high promontory; like a living star beaming out in solitude over these great stone foundations. The contrast is keen between this Solitary One and the crowds assembled under the portal, where all is brimmed with moving, sculptured figures.

I draw nearer again, then step back to the left, trying to situate the beauty of this adorable being. Now and then I understand.

The head seems like a winged sphere. The draperies are admirably supple, surpliced over tunics.

What a frame the powerful repose of the buttresses make for it!

From the height of his solitude the Angel of Chartres, in the attitude of an annunciator, views the city with joy.

He wears time on his breast and offers himself in profile, the body effaced, hovering like an acanthus leaf.

How chaste this body is! This is not the Victory of Samothrace who voluptuously shows herself, nude beneath the thinly pasted veil of draperies. Here modesty reigns. The garment comments austerely upon the forms without ever depriving them of their grace; only a

216 · TOULOUSE

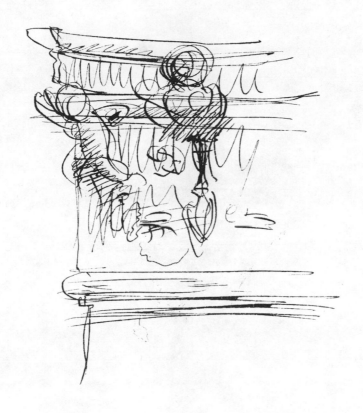

218 · BLOIS

CAEN · 219

220 · AFTER MICHELANGELO

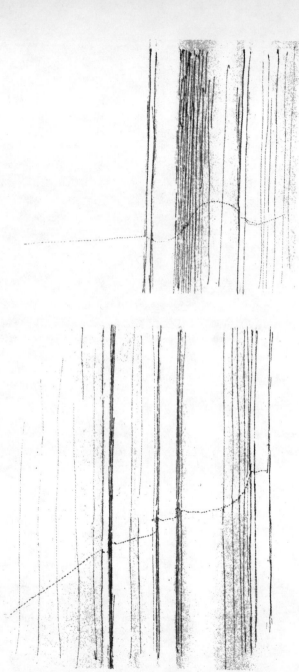

grave motive could cause a leg or an arm to advance to make a projection.

The Angel is a point on the lower part of this immense foundation, like a star in the still obscure firmament. His profile is pious and full of wisdom. He brings the Summation of all philosophies. Time is written upon him like a sentence upon the page of a book. With what self-recollection he holds and shows us time, time that wounds and that kills!

The profound significance of this gesture is the benevolent, vigilant intention of the sculptor who found and willed it. A sundial is a regulating force: God directs us as it does, ceaselessly intervening in our life by the sun's mediation. This Angel therefore wears upon his breast the law and the measure that come from the sun and from God. Man's daily task becomes divine by being ruled according to the vibrations of that divine light.

Or else, might this Angel be a sphinx? Does he ask us the meaning of time? No! he protects the city. His beauty brings a sense of equilibrium to my soul that rises toward him.

(*Much later.*)
What mirage appears in my mind?
I return once again and, arriving, I lift my eyes: *this Angel of Chartres is a Cambodian figure!*

Never did I have an impression neighboring on this one; truly I see this astonishing figure for the first time. Or at least I see it not as I had seen it to this day.

This means there are many ways of seeing a beautiful thing. As new profiles appear when one moves, so a masterpiece is transformed in us according to the movement it has provoked in our mind; this movement, which is not isolated in our life, adds to all our feelings the impression of the masterpiece that we keep, and this impression lives by our life, is colored according to other impressions that life brings us, and thanks to which we discover, between two expressions very distant one from the other, secret but real analogies.

Between two pilgrimages to Chartres, I had seen the Cambodian dancers;* I had assiduously studied them in Paris (at Pré-Catelan) and in Marseilles (at the Villa des Glycines) with paper on my knee and a pencil in my hand, amazed by their singular beauty and by the great character of their dance. What astonished and delighted me above all was to find in this art of the Far East, unknown to me until

* This was during the summer of 1906. In the July 28th issue of *L'Illustration*, I find my impressions transcribed by M. Georges Bois, Inspector of Professional Education in Indo-China, delegate of Beaux Arts to the Colonial Exposition in Marseilles where I had followed the dancers of King Sisowath. (Rodin's footnote.)

then, the very principles of the Antique. Before very ancient sculpture fragments, so ancient that one would be at a loss to assign them a date, thought gropes backward for thousands of years, seeking their origins: and all at once living nature appears, and it is as if these old stones had come to life! All that I admired in antique marbles, these Cambodians gave me, adding thereto the unknown and the lithe pliancy of the Far East. What enchantment to verify humanity's faithfulness to itself throughout time and space! But to this faithfulness there is an essential condition: that the traditional and religious sentiment be preserved. I have always confounded religious art and art; for when religion is lost, art is also lost; all masterpieces, Greek, Roman, all our own, are religious. In fact these dances are religious because they are art; their rhythm is a rite, and it is the purity of the rite which assures the purity of the rhythm. It is because King Sisowath and his daughter Samphoudry, directress of the royal ballet, take a jealous care to preserve the most strict orthodoxy in these dances that they have remained beautiful. The same thought had safeguarded art at Athens, at Chartres, and in Cambodia, everywhere, varying only by the formula of the dogma; moreover these variations themselves attenuate each other thanks to the kinship between human forms and gestures in all latitudes.

As I had recognized antique beauty in the Cambodian dances, a short while after my sojourn at Marseilles, I recognized Cambodian beauty at Chartres in the attitude of the great Angel, which indeed is not very much removed from a dance attitude. The analogy between all beautiful human expressions of all times justifies and exalts the artist's profound belief in the unity of nature. The various religions, in accord on this point, were like guardians of the great harmonious pantomimes by which human nature expresses its joys, its anguish, its certitudes. The Far West and the Far East in their superior productions, those in which the artist expressed the essential part of man, were obliged to draw closer together.

With what authority this annunciator surges from the depth of ancient times to come to us! He is more modern than we, having more life, freshness, and energy.

In his stance of a messenger, he leans forward slightly, and this movement evokes that of a hawk about to take flight. In this detail one recognizes an inflection dear to Gothic art, this movement of reverence that forms a hook. The profile changes at the time of the Renaissance to express desire and voluptuousness. From ascetic it becomes, with Michelangelo, rich and full.

To the Angel, Gothic art bequeaths the grandiose simplicity of tranquil order and admirable slowness, the combined charms of the dance and of architecture. Modesty confers majesty, a deep meaning to all the gestures of the figure and to all the details of the composition. This Angel, truly celestial, itself a luminary, holds the sundial as if it were a star. One thinks, in looking at this figure, that time is the result of the silent procession of stars in the firmament.

Beautiful being without sex, siren, Angel, you are adorable in grace, you possess the limber, yielding line, the almost oblique poise of the dance, the equilibrium that the eye adores with melancholy, that speaks of interlacing and of instability!

You were conceived by heroic minds. You are the last vestige of a sublime century.

Readers, go to see the Angel of Chartres.
It is still there; for how many days?

VII · THIS TIME I have only approached the Cathedral. From afar one sees this Being gather itself and become erect in its full-blown unity.

This masterpiece, shining over the indifferent city, borrows innovation and perpetual regeneration from the air in which it vibrates. All the hours of the day clothe, adorn, and glorify it.

What an inexhaustible source of marvels is French genius! Here I recognize the gentle obstination of the peasant genius of our race.

With this genius the climate collaborates. The French soul and the French climate operate according to the same principles. Both enfold the great monument in a diaphanous veil. It is this powerful means which prevents the details from troubling the essential lines by complicating them, and this pleasant daily mist that rises in the morning returns at evening and sometimes persists throughout the day.

Of the two towers at Chartres, one is Romanesque, the other is Gothic. At the base of the ornamented tower, the buttresses have but one projection, while those of the simple tower are mighty and bold.

The ornamented tower is of silver, but the unornamented is of gold.

My eye perceives the interlacing of stone trees that unite at the top like the branches of an enchanted forest, like hands that cross their fingers to protect a tabernacle.

Might Chartres perish? I am unwilling to believe that. The Cathedral waits for other generations worthy of understanding it.

Chartres waits, soaring proudly from certainty to certainty, witnessing to us that in certain great hours the human spirit revives, returns to a serene and tranquil order and then creates Beauty *for always.*

CHAPTER THIRTEEN

Ornaments

THE DECORATION of our churches is the work of centuries, the slow, meditative collaboration of several currents. Here man seems to have obeyed mysterious influences, laws that he *could not* transgress. He has made these works of art as the bee makes its honey, by a happy fatality.

With one difference, however. Upon a given theme man varies but exhausts himself, while the docile beasts repeat themselves tirelessly. When man reaches the end of one of his ways, there is decadence, natural night; this process was as necessary as day itself. Humanity would perish if it always used its genius in the same way, if it knew no repose of change, if it did not submit to the alternatives of death and of rebirth, to which the science of our epoch attests. In any event, it is sure that man reaches repose by being spent, and we, in our history, have reached such a phase. How slowly regeneration comes!

How many studies to recapture ancient thought in its purity! This requires an excavation not in the earth, but in the sky for, although offered to the sight of all, although in full light, that thought remains more profoundly buried than if there were need to struggle for it in the bowels of the earth. One may say that today light makes a winding sheet of all that beauty.

What is most difficult is to think, not with the primitive ingenuity of childhood, but with tradition, with acquired power, with all the resulting, hoarded treasure of thought. Indeed, the human mind cannot go very far except on this condition: that the thought of the individual be added, with patience and silence, to the thought of generations.

But modern man no longer takes account of the thought of generations.

The art of the Middle Ages, in its ornamentation as well as in its constructions, derives from nature. It is therefore always to nature that one must go for an understanding of that art.

See Reims: in its tapestries we find the same color, leaves, and flowers as in its capitals. This is true of all the Cathedrals.

Then let us give ourselves the joy of studying these flowers in nature, that we may have a just notion of the resources which the decorator of living stones required of them. He penetrated the life of flowers by contemplating their forms, by analyzing their joys and their sorrows, their virtues and their weaknesses. These are our sorrows and our virtues.

So flowers have given the Cathedral.

To be convinced, go into the country and open your eyes.

At each step you will have a lesson in architecture. Men of yore looked before us and understood. They sought the plant in the stone and now we find their immortal stones in the eternal flowers. And (is this not the greatest homage they could have hoped for?) nature, although certainly without taking account of our dates, ceaselessly speaks to us of the 12th century, of the 15th, of the 14th, of the 18th. This is because nature takes it upon herself to defend from all criticism the anonymous artists of those great epochs.

For me, these beautiful studies in the open air are beneficial. My room hurts me as shoes a size too small would hurt my feet. And how much more the city, the new city! It is in the fresh air of the fields and the woods, I must repeat, that I have learned all that I know.

The flowering fields of Verrières.

As if thrown all at once into this immense garden in the beautiful sunshine, I feel myself live through my eyes a new, more intense, and unknown life. But so much splendor makes me dizzy. These flowers that a horticulturist grows for the seeds in massive squares filled with plants all alike, these juxtaposed layers of color, create an impression of stained glass and make me live with them.

It is too radiant. My powers are insufficient. I cannot endure the sudden burst of this beauty, of this motionless beauty!

I run for refuge to shelter myself in the simple greenery where a fresh breeze, a zephyr, gently makes the leaves of my notebook tremble.

My intimidated eyes have nevertheless received and retain the impression of this stupefying magnificence. Only fifteen days ago it was almost winter, and suddenly all is burgeoning, the clouds and the trees like the flowers. This is a mad abundance, a turmoil of youth! Dazzling opulence. One dare not choose among so many treasures. For study, one needs a more restricted field.

In one flower almost all flowers are given. In the least walk through the country, it is nature as a whole that one meets, and all grassy ways are the paths of paradise.

To be sure, I am only a botanist who has missed his calling. Nevertheless I understand in my way. While "autos" spread their noise and their dust from the roads, I study, bent to the wild flowers of my path.

What curious, varied, and innumerable expressions are available to an artist!

On unequal planes, all flowers are equal; the small and the large have the same dignity.

It seems that in the morning it is easier to distinguish between them by the tips of the stems. This is the moment when flowers turn their backs to us so gracefully!

There are some that shine in splendor when they spread the ornament of their petals. Ah! floral ornament, what priceless counsel to sculptors!

Many plants imitate birds by flying in place. Attached to the stem, but very separated from each other, the leaves flutter.

Other leaves hang like flags at half mast. Still others are like cloths suspended from windows.

Little flowers that I have met in the gardens and woods, you have allowed me to make such observations as you granted to sculptors and stained-glass workers during the time of beautiful ornaments.

These two leaves, one at the right, the other at the left, pucker, become fluted, and join together. At their base grow two others, then two still smaller ones, and so on. They cast up from their hearts two small stalks that separate, carrying two flowers, two buds, and a group of smaller buds.

How precious are the veins of these leaves like delicate fans! And they are only wayside plants.

A little rose window of chalices. Flowerettes around a somber flower.

Certain wildflowers have helmets like Minerva.

The fibers of plants begin in delicate and clearly defined nerves following the principle of the stalk, springing up and entering the leaf as they run without stopping.

These leaves that fold back, that make a half turn upon themselves, that close at one-third, and then allow their edges to escape and be regathered. The flounce of a dress.
The stem that carries them is grooved like a column.
Boughs toss this way and that expressing various sentiments which never forget to be graceful.

These felled trees, outstretched, are moldings. Certainly their value is Gothic: expressed in the round.

Its whole root was in my hand. But communication with the earth was interrupted. Love cannot accept separation. Why should we be astonished that it was dead in less than half an hour? Could we live longer than this plant, far from the elements necessary for our life?

When a leaf is going to die, its partitioned surface becomes more sensitive, more salient, like the veins of an old man. It twists about itself and shrinks. But these transformations leave it its beauty, and its morbid modelings are those of a Gioconda.
Then it lets go and falls without resistance.

See, these flowers are in a state of catalepsy. When the leaf grows old, it has the aspect of an artificial flower. Its soul has evaporated. Always in this manner a flower stiffens, hardens before reaching madness, the death of the petals.
In youth, the flower draws in, assembles its petals, hiding its heart. In age, lamentable; if one holds it straight up, it falls, the petals outspread. But in dying it produces life.
Is society transformed in the same manner? We believe that all is lost and do not see the good, the work that prepares the fruit, as our death or our illness produce life or health.

When flowers fade they lose reciprocal respect, they touch each other, jostle and fall over one another. In good health they always keep a distance between them.

They hold themselves upright, but with flexible elasticity, with I know not what of an airiness, something like the elastic and smilingly balanced equilibrium of a dancer who seeks the homage that she calls forth. What uninsistent beauty and always quick to offer itself!

I believe they are proud of their sovereignty and I adore their self-esteem.

Two ailing flowers: one leans over the other in passing in front of it, and this one upholds her sister, itself bending also. There is sadness and tenderness here.

At the point where the stem is noded and sends out its digitation into membranes, the leaf embraces the stem, then, assured of a solid point of leverage, throws itself backward.

Gable ends are always formed like the apexes of plants.

Tulips.

They fling themselves, they spread out like happy courtesans; with a free movement, they bare their hearts which may not be chaste, but are indeed adorable.

This one, fallen, the "muzzle" wide open, has fainted.

That other one hangs in a plumb line. Its shuddering of distress, which I see despite its immobility, mark the madness of the flower; old age.

The most wealthy of the three Magi and the Queen of Sheba were not more sumptuously attired than this tulip of mixed gold and red.

And this, also gold and red in another design, is this a bird of the Islands? Is it not rather the wing of the Archangel Gabriel?

And in almost all I seem to find the gesture of a Sappho, the gesture that provokes and that gives. It persists even in those that have fainted, that hang their heads before them. They also seem to be colored bubbles floating in air.

And here are some that are appalling: these blood-red tulips streaked with gold are like flayed living flesh in full sunlight; in places they give the feeling of spoiled meat. These thongs, so delicately lacy, and lately so beautiful, are now rotted fibrous things. No more yellow-gold at the heart. A horrible wound of coagulated blood, a morsel of carrion, this red as of a disease that burns, this mucus that oozes. Lamentable flower that frightens us! And yet it is not dead; it suffers the transformation necessary to fructification. Is this the image of our death?

In certain tulips there is a whole marvelous sunset.
Between their petals one makes out a bleeding crucifix.

As for this one, it has lost its shape. Life is concentrated in the stem from which the flower droops sadly. Its pistils protrude beyond the petals like the paws of a lizard. But the flower still has its bursting eucharistic reds, gleaming as if these petals had been carefully brushed. This tulip has the richness of Oriental silks, of silks from Genoa.

Lacy tulips. Their red and yellow petals are like incendiary flames; curly at places, they suggest fire tormented by wind.

For there are flowers that burn. These are in full incandescence. Leaning out of the vase that supports their stalks, these tulips blaze in the air. One might be looking at flames driven by a gale that comes from all sides.

And there are flowers that cast spells. Do they not project a fluid?

It is particularly to its leaves that the white daisy has entrusted its beauty. While the stalk rises, the leaf is designed at first as a notch, then higher two more larger notches, and each one of these has the form of a little tongue.

The privileged leaves will have the joy of encircling the pride of the whole plant: the bud, which is already superb in its transitory planes and will be a flower that is very beautiful in its simplicity.

The daisy that resembles the sun is the flower of children and of lovers. The lover gives it to poets and to artists.

In its mounting leaves, the daisy simulates the form of an open-work vase in wrought iron. It curls up when it bends, faded. It leans, and when it is about to fall, it is a little hand, a small paw with too many curled fingers. Several faded daisies: little cut-out valances.

When young and fresh, this flower is an admirable principle of decoration. All ornament makers of the best epochs have studied it. Its leaf is the French acanthus.

The lily-of-the-valley flowers at the same time as the cowslip because the beauty of these two flowers destines them for symmetrical places in the bouquet of the beautiful season.

Each one of them is very feminine.

Another woodland flower evokes a flat-bottomed canoe with its rowers. It bends an elbow to turn back upon itself.

I am not familiar with this plant whose leaves are all ink stained. Might this be the scholar's flower? Or the scribe's?

The violet leaf is in the form of a heart.

Honeysuckle has little green leaves like lentil leaves; its stem has four angles, like the church of Saint Gudule.*

* *Translator's note:* In Belgium.

This little clover, that has been ironed at this very instant, remains pleated in the manner of holy vestments.

Dandelion, wood sorrel, lance head, halberd.

The petals of this blue pansy are a dark blue velvet and cream-colored silk chasuble.

The lilacs are so fresh! They seem to offer a glimpse of beautiful weather.
Their leaves, a little wavy with inconsistent shadows, are full of vigor.

The carnation is the flower of Louis XV. It was worn in knotted ribbon on slippers. But earlier the Gothics carved it where the arcs of the vaulting surfaces meet.

This dandelion shows us all that it has in its belly! It thinks only of reproduction.

The wild forget-me-not has a slightly dizzy air. It has not much memory; it is too small.

The weed: oriflamme, golden flame, a bright and glorious banner, inspiring courage and devotion.

The leaf of the cherry tree has vivid touches on its upper surface. This is an essentially Gothic leaf; you will often find it in the plaster casts of the Trocadero museum.*

The plantain, that weed of "coupasse" that is used for cuttings,† is a spear upheld on both sides. Its leaf is singed.

This eye of the anemone is angry and bloody. I know nothing more heart gripping than this flower. The one I am looking at is at the critical age; it is covered with fine wrinkles; its petals are as if disjointed; it is going to fall. The Persian vase in which I have placed it, blue, white, and cream, makes for it a worthy tomb. Its sisters in full bloom are designs for rose windows.

This large flower, of the violet color that I love in certain stained-glass windows of Notre Dame, touches me like a memory, especially now that we are returning to God, this flower and I. Its sad heart, where a black bud is forming, is also encircled by a black crown

*Translator's note: Now the Musée des Monuments Historiques.
† Translator's note: Used to mix with or "to cut" certain medicines.

which the petals exaggerate, and these violet petals make the window seem to stand before the light. This flower is a widow.

All my flowers are there, beneath my eyes, answering my call.

Yesterday I saw among them arms, hands, and profiles.

Today they draw themselves up like the branches of candelabra, offering to hold lights. A single one has fallen and hangs like a dead snake.

There is no doubt that the beauty of flowers and their movements express thoughts; as our own movements and our beauty. But flowers speak in chorus; they have only a collective consciousness, only unanimous thought.

Thus they command us not to lose the feeling of the whole, even while we take advantage of the charming details that they allow us to see.

All these flowers, and many others, indeed all others, have served as models for sculptors and stained-glass workers. As the painter-stained-glass worker took his hues from them, the sculptor took his harmonious joinings.

Glass worker, you have crucified the flowers in your blood-red windows of the Passion.

CHAPTER FOURTEEN

Last Testament

I speak in my last moments to revive vanished centuries and recall
them to view. I am like a breath in a clarion that amplifies the sound.
I resign myself to the death of these buildings as to my own death.
Here I make my last testament.

The laws that I express are those of instinct. They have no need of grammar, that children's nurse.

This book does not dissect the Cathedral but offers it, alive, to life.

The spirit upon a ground of intelligence: beautiful bas-relief.

The intelligence draws, but it is the heart that models.*

* *Translator's note:* A number of the notes of this section and the previous one appear, differently expressed, in Gustave Coquiot's three books on Rodin.

The ignorant or indifferent man, by only looking at beautiful things, destroys them.

Man is satisfied to live on the edge of his dreams. He neglects the realities that are so beautiful!

An old, bent woman lifts her head and looks at me; then she continues to glean by small handfulls. I, too, am a gleaner, the happy gleaner of ancient times, or rather a student, an old apprentice of the noble companions of long ago. Do I not see all about me in the lie that our century gives them, proof that they were right?

The race returns to its source! How I feel within me the joy of those artists of past centuries and their fertile simplicity! Sensitive hearts that found in art, not luxury, but the very principle of their life.

Ah! the Secret! Not everyone loves it. I do not ask, as Goethe did, for "more light"; I would not lose the benefit of the marvelous grotto where all the Thousand and One Nights are found; I stop myself there.

A prodigious beauty envelopes all, like a tissue, like a protecting shield.

There is no chaos in the human body, model of all things, point of departure and culmination of all.

Repetition and regularity constitute the ground of beautiful things. This is a law. Romanesque and Gothic art are ruled by it: columns, banisters, extensors, and these moldings.

The banister and lacework are Gothic. Later, numerous scrolls will replace the Gothic clover in the tympanum.

Who can believe in progress? Time, like the earth, mounts and descends; its ellipse, during the course of a century, sweeps along the preceding century, through both good and evil, through day and night. We should long ago have been gods if the theory of indefinite progress were true.

I love man's effort which, by regular repetitions, is continually augmented. This repeated movement is the enactment of a battle, and these Cathedral columns multiply their grace by following and uniting with each other.

FROM NATURE · *The study of nature and the study of great works accomplished by man's genius bring the spirit to the same con-*

clusions. A few words about the living Model are therefore not out of place here: they prepare for an understanding of sculpture as moldings* prepare for an understanding of architecture.

(Reclining figure.)

I see that this beautiful person feels the movement, the arousing of thought that she provokes while in her likeness a statue is being sketched in the artist's mind.

He has not taken a modeling stand, he is not installed for work, but did he not call this model with the intention of working from her?

This arm, this bust surprised him. Nevertheless he had guessed their beauty. His eye runs over the whole, over the details, then returns to the movement of a very beautiful style remarked in the first place, which he recognizes in its larger expression and it is this, precisely, that he studies.

It is then that he sees all that can be seen for sculpture. For a dress is a sack, just that and nothing more. An artist needs to see more. And what can he see? Always the same splendor: always life recommencing and renewing itself with each pulsation.

* *Translator's note:* The French word here is *moulage* (casting), but Rodin's thought on that subject makes that seem a misreading of his word *moulure*, as defined on pages 274-275 and elsewhere.

What dazzlement, a woman who disrobes! It is as the sun piercing the clouds!

At first sight this body seen as a whole is a blow, a commotion.

Like an arrow, the eye for a moment surprised, glances off.

In each model, nature is present in its entirety, and the eye that knows how to see discovers and follows it so far! Follows it especially to what most persons do not know how to see: the unknown depths, the foundations of life. Above elegance there is grace, above grace, the modeling. But all such surpasses words. Of modeling we say that it is tender, but it is powerfully tender. Words are lacking.*

Yes, I have studied and understood form. That can be learned, but the genius of form remains ever to be studied.

This morsel of living antiquity, with the same forms as in the Antique, is admirable reclining here on this sofa. A brown monk's

* *Translator's note:* Surprising variations of this paragraph and of the next two pages appear in *Sculptures Çivaïtes* by A. Rodin, A. Coomaraswamy, Brussels and Paris, 1921.

robe modeled by intense light, accompanies this body. The austere ardor that the robe expressed in prayer, its tone of passion, it imparts to the voluptuous flesh whose royal lines it veils.

Antiquity never found a drapery in this color of a dead leaf, which is more beautiful than red.

This corner of the mouth, this line at first thin that turns, enlarging while undulating, recalls the antique dolphin.

These lips are like a pool of pleasure shared by the so-noble and palpitating nostrils.

The mouth glides in damp delight, sinuous as a serpent. The eyes are swollen, closed by the seam of the lashes.

Words in motion, issuing from the lips, are shaped by their delicious undulation.

Eyes, that have but a corner in which to hide, are couched in the purity of lines and in the tranquility of stars.

Like a fallen fruit, this face thrown back, with its horizontal eye that sees vaguely yet allows itself to be seen, that calls.

All the curves say and constantly repeat the same sweetness; the concerted expression of an infinite world. For this eye, like a sun of intelligence and love, gives life and does not hold it back. However, this eye and this mouth understand one another.

Charming profile, but profile lost, in which the expression completes and effaces itself to allow the cheeks to merge into tendons of the neck.

(Figure lighted from the side.)
With what joy the intellect molds over this supple beauty as plaster exactly follows the contours of form in order to reproduce it faithfully!

In shadow, chiaroscuro models with so much truth! There, in its fullness, the grace of a voluptuous Psyche is revealed. But the line of the modeling is drawn with luminous strokes that follow the whole side of the torso and of the thigh.

Three-fold peach, thrice downy! This billowing line is full of its own roundness, its own clarity.

Garlands of shadows oscillate from the shoulder to the hip, and to the protruding forms of the thigh.

Somnolent flesh, tranquil lake.
Open sea where ardor's vibrations fade away.
Full, white flesh.

(*Kneeling woman bending to the side.*)

Her two joined hands pray; they separate the breasts and the abdomen.

This gesture rivals the grace of the Medici Venus, whose hands hide the secrets of her beauty. This living Venus protects herself by this morbid prayer.

With what extraordinary passion shadow embraces this beautiful body! The hands, touched by light, imprint themselves upon this delicious fruit whose shadow hides the eloquent mystery, while allowing it to be guessed.

Without modeling in depth, the contour could not be rich and supple as it is; it would be dry.

The beautiful straight shadow of this woman on her knees, this vertical shadow that divides the torso in two, falls in crossing over the two thighs, taking possession of half of one and the whole of the other. Opposition between the cast shadow and the chiaroscuro, the one giving life to the other.

The prize of beauty belongs in fact to no one woman, but is shared by all. Each one is fulfilled in her personal beauty as a fruit ripens according to the laws of its kind.

As for me, it is a long time since I knew what an "academy" is but I know what a woman is, or a flower, against whom no one has yet committed the outrage of making them academic.

ARCHITECTURE · THE IMMENSE ROOFS of Cathedrals are as reposeful as landscapes.

Trees bring order and animation to everything, and imposing architecture lends itself to them.

These trees, like archangels, bow their heads to one another, their wings unfurled, vertical against the sky.

This deep and eloquent black is no longer black; it is a food of the grand style: it is depth, the active principle of the beauty of the Middle Ages and of all ages.

To all centuries preceding ours, this profound force has given the style which is declined in a thousand varieties up to Louis XVI, and even including the Empire.

Gothic style was France's benefactor to about 1820. Its traces are still among certain of our peasants who have kept the black costume and the bonnet worn by figures that ornament our Cathedrals.

What is beautiful in landscape is also what is beautiful in architecture. It is the air, which no one appreciates: it is depth. Depth seduces the soul and sends it where it will.

This swelling stem is moved by a new sensation, the same as that of a young girl who feels the rounding out of her breasts.

The procession is the soul of bas-relief. It is an inscription, a temple border, a frieze or an ornament.
And columns are also inspired by the procession.

Beauvais.
In leaving the Cathedral I pause under the porch and, with head raised and thrown back, I gaze at the soaring of the arch that surmounts the tympanum. Unexpected and intense effect. This is the upheaval of creation. It is chaos. It is also the Last Judgment. On account of ornaments that overflow the arch, the architecture seems unsealed: parts mount up, others fall down. This has the grandeur of a cataclysm. To the material upheaval of its ordering is added that of the man who gazes in an odd position, a little obliquely from three-quarters and with deep inner distress. It is nevertheless beautiful! Impetuous moment.

The Cathedral of Chartres is in my mind at this moment, and there it falls in with the Mass by Mozart where divine sounds stream from all sides. Graceful effects, numberless lights.

And at the same time memories of my youth come to mind. In those days I was admitted only where admission was free, and yet I harvested millions of thoughts, silver from heaven.

Before this Cathedral, my first impression is total astonishment. The mind strives to comprehend the past and to penetrate it with new sight. It calls for conclusions that would generalize earlier studies, thus attempting to approach the Sphinx.

These intersections of forces!
Above are curves, rules, palpitations of the stone against a murky sky where the imagination gropes and glimpses.

These types of apses that are linked with each other by a pavement, this crumbling that I admire, crumbling of times and of Parthenons, more in ruins at night, more advanced in disaster by two centuries.

The sun comes to sleep in this church over these tiles, these moldings, these columns, over this entirety that calls to life and holds it within the eye's range. This abandoned church is like its epitaphs: living in death, its continuance overhangs the centuries.

Its beauty, nonetheless, is revealed only to those who make themselves like its meditative creators. One does not lend admiration; it is personal. Seven hundred years ago these stones obeyed the Master's conception, which we strive to discover, to reinvent.

Without purity you can enter here; but without intelligence, no; not here where it is known how to weave the sun's rays and enhance their value.

Without the least doubt, the beauty of Reims *exists* and reaches us even when the failing light no longer allows us to see it. Foreknowledge reveals it to us, intuition, instinct, those vigil keepers! To the eye all is confused, but the few points that one still sees suffice to fix it in the mind and make it conform. Even at midday when the building is fully lighted, the eye would not see more than at night without the help of the soul.

The eye is a simple camera; the artist is the brain.

The sublime is at my window, indecipherable. I wait for night to enter the interior and to understand.

Close observation still reveals a regularity in this grandeur. Such order must be restored to my own mind.

At least I can already enjoy this imposing wealth of greyness.

Strong joists carry the vault of stalactites. Beehives where the great artists of the Renaissance will carve Last Judgments, and later Jupiters, Psyches, Veronicas, where the arcs recall astronomy, the heavenly vaults, and those celestial geometries whose ellipses Dante has described.

In these ancient monuments the belfry is penetrated by gables. Moreover all the elements of the building interpenetrate without being based upon a uniform line of departure.

I have never seen the sun so gloriously manifested as in the arching curves of the portal at Reims. The Virgin triumphs in the high pediment; the coronation of Woman, divine gesture to which, with the angels, all men concur as enraptured servants. The triumph of gentleness, apotheosis of obedience; masterpiece of advice to women.

This radiant one holds her child, the Son of God. And is not the child of every woman always the son of God?

Caen.

Caen was an organized capital of ancient beauty.

It has masterpieces of the first order in which triumphs a Renaissance issued from the Gothic.

What admirable profusion of spirit!

The French spirit is at its height of power in Gothic art. It becomes impoverished but it will be regularized, to excess, perhaps, with the Italian Renaissance.

The baldachin of Caen (bronze and marble of the Italian Renaissance) is completely beautiful. High up are an angel and cherubim. This is an opera stage set, but what magnificence! These galleries, these balconies, the rectitude of this architecture, this dance step with the delicacy of wrought iron.

But today Caen takes its orders from Paris, and all that comes from there is thin and tasteless. This is the lesson of those architectural revolutionaries who glue everything together again, supposedly, but in reality they destroy everything. They stifle the monuments, they alter the face of French art, they dishonor and annihilate it.

Complicity of the times. It was necessary to pass through a whole century of aberrations and ruins in order that the 20th century might reascend to the pure source. But for the 20th century to accomplish that salutary work, profound changes must come about in mores.

See, for example, the restoration of the *chevet* of Saint Peter: it could be mistaken for an imitation of a piece of furniture from the Saint Antoine neighborhood.

The Church of Cambronne (Romanesque).

The lower part begins with a heavy pillar; shadowed group. The perspective is gently modeled; no hardness; the light is honied; the ogives register without violence; the columns that carry the weight are executed with as much tenderness as force. The patinas recall the Antique.

Thus there is but one curve since the Greeks! One only that is beautiful, whichever language the styles may speak.

These daises up high, magnificence of ornamentation.

The heads of these saints are adorned with the grace of natural imagination as with tiaras.

These architectures, these ornaments smile discreetly.

This is almost a secret life: we cannot penetrate into this closed and finished circle.

Buttresses are like bridges, aqueducts that cross and pass, grey forms; transversal arcades which the light reaches only as grey tones.

One part of the nave, lighted, leans over the other which is in full shadow, which hides itself, fixed eternally.

These so-tall columns, slightly bending back, describe a unique circular movement which defends them from the assault of the centuries.

The architect weighs and lengthens lines, giving them the pride of movement which carries them farther over the horizon: faithful sphinxes, trailing vines, garlands; stations of our thought, first attempts, preludes on the part of creation that is dispensed to us.

The architectural system of the Middle Ages is the same as that of Antiquity: identical motif here and there, countless aspects of Venus, always moving with life.

Architecture consists in the obedience of the details, and of the whole, to the generating line of the contours.

The line of force is the same in the Romanesque as in other styles. Forms that differ in appearance harmonize in their result. The effect sums up the whole in the mass of French styles.

The thrust of masses must coincide with the subject and also absorb it. A plane does not end because the subject ends, but because the mass has accomplished its movement. If this movement has not completed its evolution, the sculpture is not finished. (I speak of true *finish*, completion which has importance above the finicky touching up of arms, legs, heads, etc.)

The movement continues when the statue has said what it intended to say. But it is not alone in speaking: the accessories answer it. The plane must overflow the sculpture in order that the plinth and the accessory may continue in the same movement.

Ornaments, draperies, or simple rocks are cast into a movement that completes the principal figure. The principal figure also is grouped with them, since from afar the subject no longer counts; there are only masses. It is certain that before making out the form of a woman on this pediment, I had to be interested in the mass of stone. I had to see it as architecture, to see how that figure emerges from the play of other masses and how it is one with them.

Next I strive to analyse the whole and the detail.

In a work of sculpture, you try to see if the form is good or bad and what the subject is. You are wrong.

General rule: Of first importance is the right relationship of masses. By that the style is revealed; by that one can judge whether the work is by a skillful or a clumsy sculptor. In a pediment one sees at once if the figures are well balanced.

Balance does not always require that the dominant mass be in the center; it may be to one side and still be in equilibrium with the whole architecture. Such is the sculpture of the 18th century, and this it is that gives lightness (for example the bas-reliefs above the windows on the façades of the Place de la Concorde and of the Legion of Honor). Also the sculptors of that time were not burdened by the subject—seasons, female figures, draped or nude, with or without cherubs. The subject did not count in the 18th century. That century was reproached for this insignificance of subject matter, which we have remedied by inventing stories, thus proving that we have lost the sense of sculpture and of architecture. Our worthy forebears were not "thinkers": they expressed themselves in all simplicity by beautiful masses and had nothing to do with our picture puzzles.*

The horizontal panels above the Chancellery windows express nothing else than this agreeable distribution of projections that go in and out of the background, appearing and disappearing with no other function than to give fullness and breadth to the sculpture that does so well on the bare wall.

Our epoch, misconstruing the laws of architecture, believed it

* *Translator's note:* Rodin developed this paragraph differently in notes he lent to Aurel for *Rodin Devant la Femme*, Maison du Livre, Paris, 1919, page 141.

could demand sculptural effects from ideas. Baneful revolution! There is nothing to hope for in that direction. We begin to return from it, late indeed.

To sum up: it is the lighting that regulates architecture. It is not the "rational," that barbarous term. The sort of pure, correct drawing, "spun out" in the manner of Ingres, without involuntary starts or shudders, is a drawing that takes no account of the plane; it is thin, hard, poor.

The Romanesque is continued in embroidery, ornaments, and festoons.

How simple it is! For example a hem, an ornamented border, Coptic or Etruscan.

The Trocadero Museum.

What astonishing beauty is preserved in the *barbarous* Romanesque reliefs! That is because the antique plane is the tissue of which they are made: faults of form cannot destroy the beauty of style.

When I was young, I found all this hideous because I looked at it with nearsighted eyes; I was ignorant like everyone else. Later, I saw what was being done in my time, and I understood who were the Barbarians.

In Romanesque days when men made a game of expressing their fantastic visions in their carved capitals and when architecture, like God's law, governed the populace and ordained rewards and punishments according to the law of symmetry, truth was inscribed on the pediment of the temple. Here is the terrible commandment of Destiny that wills birth and death, which God Himself obeys, this God of the fearsome tympanum, this Judge surrounded by His Assyrian lion, by His angel in a pleated tunic, and by His bellowing bull.

It is certain that Byzantine art is connected with that of India and of China. Romanesque art is still marked by that connection.

There is no black in Romanesque and Gothic art of the 13th century except as strokes of emphasis in the draperies. With what intelligence these infrequent blacks are dispensed!

In the First Renaissance there is a profusion of small ornaments, useless, one is tempted to say. They come from the generosity of a rich heart that does not economize, that does not choose marble and gold to express itself, but is content with stone and sends that up to the vaults in embroidered festoons. Art, at its dawning, has no need for richness. Michelangelo's chapel in Florence kills the chapel of the cardinals.

It is when the wounded soul begins to suffer the approaches of evening that it uses rich material like, for example, the Second Renaissance.*

Wood and stone preceded bronze. Colored marble, lapis lazuli, precious stones appear when an epoch has already passed its highest expression.

Chandeliers, candelabra that elevate the light, accompanying leaves, reclothing and polishing the general form of the edifice, lace-work in tiers, stalactites that fall from the sky, all these make a delicious cage, deliciously ornamented and always with method, with this same and unique method thanks to which a son perpetuates his ancestor, a style follows a style, and the newly acquired devolves from the old. Destiny flowers. Obedient man does not take the risk of seeking novelty, but pursues the century-old movement. All flows from one century to another like a river of beauty without eddies, without waterfalls, without violence, *without disorganization.* The word "originality" has yet to be found. The very idea that this word translates does not exist in any mind. The artist follows the logical development of the beautiful and does not needlessly exceed this range. The repercussions, the vibrations spread according to the law of nature, like the sound of a bell.

Translator's note: Like Viollet-le-Duc, Rodin saw 12th and 13th century Gothic as the First French Renaissance, and that of the 16th as the Second.

A Cathedral is a bond that unites all. It is the tie, the pact of civilization.

It is easy to discuss a marvel, easier still to spoil it.

Faith civilized the Barbarians that we were; by repulsing it, we become Barbarians once more.

The Mass (Cathedral of Limoges).

The opening prayers of the Mass make the sound of water in the fonts, purifying water. They are recited in a single tone with unobtrusiveness. What an explosion later when God arrives!

Child chorister; angelic harmony, song imitating the nightingale.

Then the voices rebound to become musically what the vault is architecturally. Music and architecture meet, cross one another, and unite in elegant melodies.

Finally the supreme Majesty enters.
Trinity. Mystery.

The priest speaks now, in a more severe voice, and the whole church answers him.

A new chant rises, a stronger rhythm; love expresses itself more loudly. All reaches me with regularity, like the distant movement of the sea. The antiphons open and underline the mystery. The organ, with muffled accents, upholds the voices.

The fiery triangles of the altar say: *Alleluia*!

The scene opens. Ah, what innocent grandeur!

The shadows, the hollows pass before me, still somber; but the church is no longer frightening as it was before the office began. This is the domination of prayer in a superb severity. My soul no longer moves in bounds. It is regularized like a centaur who contains and governs himself.

The voices are hushed with piety. Latin syllables, beloved tongue.

From afar the voice of the Gospel reaches me, the very voice of the columns. Pure waves of feminine voices, childlike: the voices of a children's choir.

And the Mass continues in silence. Then the priest takes up the word again and with joy I recognize the sonorous language of Rome.

The organ causes a short upheaval, a multitude of voices enclosed beneath great mounting waves. Ah Mozart, here are your masters!

Adorable art, dear to my soul! The organ assembles and binds together our scattered thoughts; then it pierces and dominates all. And the voices still rise and are dispersed. Religious delirium.

New faith: *Amen! In saecula saeculorum!*

Supermen transformed by prayer; they implore with the melodies of Adonis. The monster Geryon that roars in the organ replies to their questions.

Great moment; Byzantine angels burn incense.

Love answers again: *Credo.* Ah, here all is love! The organ seems to throw flowers along the way. What living purity!

The last syllables have been uttered. Little bells are sounded, and the monster roars again. At intervals, between clamorings, the sweet voices of the cantors reverberate.

What submission in that prolonged *Amen*!

The vault is now still higher: immense.

Crescendo. Pure, ultracelestial voices.

Ah yes, what glory to submit our spirit to the rule that can reform it! Moving countenance of the past.

Now the Cathedral envelopes and binds the congregation.

The Mass is over. There remain only the precious vessels and this profound architecture where the immortal act is accomplished, the act of faith.

As the faithful withdraw, the organ accompanies them with the whole protestation of the great centuries. It is at this moment that Bach and Beethoven are interpolated.

Bound sheaves after the reaping. Silence. The Mystery is accomplished. God is sacrificed, as daily, following His example, are the men of genius whom He inspires.

Superior works are still found in our provincial cities that are not yet internationalized.

I propose that pilgrimages be made to all monuments in the open air that have been spared restoration: churches, castles, fountains, etc.

People who dabble in restoration, not understanding the French smile, freeze and alter it.

Why have these restored moldings, made of such tender stone, the hardness of iron? Why is tenderness no longer mingled with strength as it used to be?

In simplicity is perfection, in coldness is impotency.
Our beliefs have been violated.
Our century is the cemetery of the beautiful centuries that built France, it is the epitaph of that which was. To create these master-pieces, required a gentle soul; such a soul France possessed.

SCULPTURE · DRAWING FROM ALL SIDES is in sculpture the incan-tation by which the soul is brought down into the stone. The result is marvelous, it gives all the profiles of the soul at the same time as those of the body.
He who has tried this system stands apart from others.

It is this drawing, this mystical conjuration of lines, that captures life.

These things have been known; they belong to us as they belonged to the Ancients, to the Gothics, to those of the Renaissance. We have a right to them.

That one should be able to capture the soul's reality in stone and imprison it for centuries! It is our desire to possess, to put in servitude, and make eternal that we place on these eyes and this mouth, which will live and speak.

Should we not know the geography of our bodies?

This breast is led by distant slopes that turn imperceptibly. All bears upon general forms that lend their lines to each other and are woven with one another. This is the concert of forms.

The intellect observes their agreement, their unity, and weighs them. These agreements are not so remote as we think, for we have divided all by the mind without being able to reconstruct.

This initial aspect of the intelligence, this synthesis of which few are capable, is ill understood by whoever has not found it for himself.

We are taught things as if they were divided, and man leaves them divided. Rare are those who consent to the patient effort required to reassemble them.

The secret of a good drawing is in the sense of its concordances: things launch into each other, interpenetrate, and clarify one another mutually. This is life's way.

The sculptor describes these things in succession, without losing the sense of their unity.

Let there be no seam, that all may appear as in a drawing made by a single stroke.

Do not forget that style in drawing is the unity obtained by study, and not by a sort of ideal inspiration. In a word, sculpture is patience.

Do you see this grace that hurries to fill all with its charms? It is the lively architecture of the 18th century, the ornamentation that one is wrong to despise, for this ornamented style is the very synthesis of architecture.

The heightening of form, that magnificent effect of modeling, seems to multiply the projections all the while affirming and augmenting the simplicity. But this result would be illusory if each "passage" did not fit in with all the others.* It is upon this unity that the quality of the modeling depends, and a sculptor would always be wrong if he did not know how to resolve this prototype of woman! † He cannot achieve unity, he cannot separate it out, except by making the sum of all the profiles.

In marbles from the Antique, all the salient points are rounded, the angles are flattened. The curves have been interpreted by the Graces. No other people than the Greeks have had this vital flexibility, this youth. France has had delicacy and wit, but perhaps it has lacked that supreme ardor of compassionate modeling. It happens sometimes in French sculpture that the delectable is meager, that delicacy is lacking in profiles, and that the ineffable lacks reality, while there is an excess of voluptuousness. The nature of form is more severe, more tranquil, and as normal as the skies.

There is no hardness in a Greek marble, that model of models. By filling in the hollows, by softening the useless and disturbing projections, since the eternal atmosphere would always end by wearing them away, the Greek artist achieved a form which participates in the environment, in the atmosphere itself. He worked with a feverish but lucid ardor and did not allow himself to be drawn into be-

*Translator's note: If all the profiles did not join together.
† Translator's note: Synthesis.

traying nature by anything empty, meager, or cold. Thus he realized that immortal work which the modern artist discovers and understands by force of study and patience twenty years after having seen it for the first time. And then he also is able to defy the marble and dedicate his work to poets.

Louvre Museum.

The divine form of the nude! With voluptuous respect my memories constantly return to the Venus of Melos, first source of nourishment for my intellect.

The perfection of these polished limbs comes to my mind when I think of the vast rooms enriched by those precious marbles. An impression of holiness as of a temple was there, and still persists. There I knew the august form that I see in the nude. With this I have purified myself. It has filled my life, my soul, and my art, which will be my soul's last resource, my final thought.

Modeling is a power ravished by study from the law of the sun's effects. Thus animated, that power participates in life, insinuating itself into a work like blood to make beauty circulate there.

This is no dead study which one may abandon and take up at will. When a tradition is once lost, it is lost for a long time; we know something about that, we who are terrified by the present anarchy, we who see masterpieces fall beneath the pickaxes of imbeciles and tyrannized over by the ignorant majority.

But haven't ignorant men a right to life? Haven't they even their usefulness in general existence? Are they not charged with making the night into which the dome and the spire must return?

Yes.

In the figurines from Tanagra there is a feminine nuance; the discreet grace of these draped limbs that express the soul's retreat is a nuance that no words could tell.

More than all, Egyptian art draws me. It is pure. The spirit's elegance engarlands all its works.

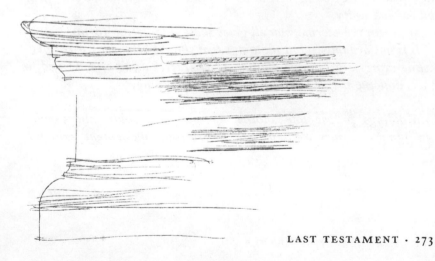

Moldings

IN SPIRIT AND ESSENCE *moldings represent and make known the whole thought of the master builder.*

Who sees this and understands it, sees the monument.

Its tenderness is that of nature herself; its life, the life of the work as a whole. Moldings contain all the architect's power and express all his thought.

Let us return to an adoration of what inspired moldings in the first place. They contrived to pour out a gentle grace, power, flexibility, and unity.

Woman, the eternal model, gives these undulating forms.

It is not ornament, but moldings that should be a rest for the eyes, while expressing in cross section the character of an epoch. And, in fact, doucine is the name of the French molding.

Moldings follow one another in orderly fashion, the slender, springing contours are developed as are those movements which at times turn from their initial line, their nuances charged with immediate expression.

Into moldings, ornament, and all architecture, the Renaissance poured the music of flesh, the adored flesh of woman and her tenderness.

Moldings are gentle symphonies.

Index of Place Names

Legion of Honor, façades of, 260
Le Châtelet-en-Brie, 31-32
Le Mans Cathedral, 14, 148 ff.
Limay, 41
Limoges Cathedral, 264
Loches, 176
Loire, river and countryside, 33-35
Loudun, 177
Louvre Museum, 167, 196, 272 f.

Magny, countryside near, 35 ff.
Mans, le, the Cathedral of, 14, 148 ff.
Mantes, 39, 42, 115 ff., 179
Marseilles, Villa des Glycines at, 222
Melun, the church at, 103
Meudon, the city of, 24, 29
  the countryside near, 89 f.
Montjavoult, the church of, 35
Montrésor, 180
Musée des Monuments Historiques.
  See Trocadéro Museum

Nevers Cathedral, 137, 138 ff.
Nîmes, the Arena at, 13
Notre Dame de Paris, the windows
  of, 241
Noyons Cathedral, 55

Orange, the Theater at, 58

Paestum, the Temple of, 73
Paris, 21, 47, 52, 98
Parthenon, the, 14, 26, 36, 61, 77
Place de la Concorde, 260
Pré-Catelan, 224

Reims, the Cathedral at, XVII, 14, 54,
  55, 160 ff., 230, 254, 255
  the statue in the Royal Square,
  171

Saint-Cloud, 27, 69
Saint-Denis, 55
Saint-Etienne of Nevers, 138 ff.
Saint Gudule, the church in Bel-
  gium, 239